WEST WICKHAM
in the
SECOND WORLD WAR

WEST WICKHAM
in the
SECOND WORLD WAR

Joyce Walker

HOLLIES PUBLICATIONS

Front cover
Funeral cortège of the five Coney Hall
AFS men killed March 1941

Back cover
VJ celebrations in Blake Recreation Ground 1945
Beckenham Journal

Other titles from Hollies Publications
West Wickham – Past into Present
The Long Alert
West Wickham and the Great War

Published by Hollies Publications
69 Hawes Lane, West Wickham, Kent BR4 0DA
First published 1990
© Joyce Walker 1990

ISBN 0 9511655 3 4

Printed and bound in the United Kingdom by
Staples Printers Rochester Limited,
Love Lane, Rochester, Kent

Remembering
Cyril Alfred Sedge
of the
Merchant Navy

Acknowledgements

The staff at the Local Studies Department of Bromley Central Library for their continued cheerful assistance

Bromley Central Library for permission to use copyright photographs

Mr. S. J. Chastney, Headmaster of Wickham Common School, for permission to quote from *Wickham Common School Jubilee 1937–1987*

Mrs. A. J. Rowlands of the Commonwealth War Graves Commission for her efficient servicing of my requests for information

Dr. Ronald Cox for allowing me to read the relevant chapters from *From Cradle to Conscription – A Schoolboy in Suburbia*, and for supplying me with the street map used for the end papers

Mr. D. J. Cozens, Headmaster of Greenhayes School, for access to the school archives

Mrs. Ivy Crier for allowing me to use family correspondence relating to Jack Crier

Croydon Advertiser for permission to use copyright photographs

My daughter, Mrs. Mary Daniels, who has helped me in the production of this book

Mr. Arthur Davie for permission to use his Infantry Roll Book

Alan de Maid for permission to use a copyright photograph

The Revd. Canon Owen Everson, vicar of St. Francis of Assisi Church, who gave me access to the church archives

Mrs. Elizabeth Gibbs for directing me to very useful contacts

Kentish Times for permission to use copyright photographs

Mr. J. S. Lomas, Headmaster of Hawes Down Junior School for permission to use the school log books

The Revd. Francis Madge, vicar of St. Mary of Nazareth Church, who gave me access to the church archives

Mr. George Plumb, photographer, who reproduced pictures from wartime newspapers

The Revd. John Poole, rector of St. John the Baptist Church, who gave me access to the church archives

The Revd. David Reep, minister at Hawes Lane Methodist Church, for access to the church archives

The Revd. Derek Richmond, minister at Emmanuel URC Church, for access to the church archives

Mr. Roy Walker, my husband, who has helped me in the production of this book

The staff at West Wickham Library for their assistance in locating books

The many kind people who have shared their memories with me. Their names are listed at the back of this book.

The following people have lent me photographs and documents:

Mrs. Alice Abbott, Mrs. Sarah Becket, Mrs. Ivy Crier, Mr. Bert Durling, Mr. Brian Etheridge, Revd. Owen Everson, Mrs. Audrey Hearne, Mrs. Pauline James, Mrs. Margaret Mayes, Mrs. Doreen Meloy, Mr. John Merigan, Mrs. Joyce Moore, Mr. Frank Preston, Mrs. Kathleen Sheridan, Mrs. Girlie Sirett, Mrs. Pauline Terry, Mr. Ron Warner, Mr. Oliver Woodman

Contents

Illustrations

Maps

Abbreviations

AA	Anti Aircraft
AB	Able Seaman
AC2	Aircraftman 2nd Class
AFS	Auxiliary Fire Service
ARP	Air Raid Precautions
ATS	Auxiliary Territorial Service
Bdr	Bombardier
BEM	British Empire Medal
Bn	Battalion
CBE	Commander of the Order of the British Empire
CD	Civil Defence
Cpl	Corporal
CPO	Chief Petty Officer
DCM	Distinguished Conduct Medal
DFC	Distinguished Flying Cross
DFM	Distinguished Flying Medal
DSM	Distinguished Service Medal
DSO	Distinguished Service Order
ENSA	Entertainments National Service Association
F/Lt	Flight Lieutenant
F/O	Flying Officer
F/Sgt	Flight Sergeant
G.I.	Government Issue (A private soldier in the US army)
HE	High explosive
KCC	Kent County Council
Kia	Killed in action
LAC	Leading Aircraftman

LDV	Local Defence Volunteer
Lt	Lieutenant
Lt Col	Lieutenant Colonel
MBE	Member of the Order of the British Empire
MC	Military Cross
MM	Military Medal
MTB	Motor Torpedo Boat
NCO	Non-commissioned Officer
NFS	National Fire Service
OBE	Officer of the Order of the British Empire
OTU	Operational Training Unit
P/O	Pilot Officer
RA	Royal Artillery
RAC	Royal Armoured Corps
RAF	Royal Air Force
RAFVR	Royal Air Force Volunteer Reserve
RAMC	Royal Army Medical Corps
RAOC	Royal Army Ordnance Corps
RASC	Royal Army Service Corps
RB	Rifle Brigade
RCS	Royal Corps of Signals
RE	Royal Engineers
RF	Royal Fusiliers ·
RN	Royal Navy
RNR	Royal Naval Reserve
RNVR	Royal Naval Volunteer Reserve
RSM	Regimental Sergeant Major
RSPCA	Royal Society for the Prevention of Cruelty to Animals
SFTS	Services Flying Training School
Sgt	Sergeant
S/L	Squadron Leader
Sub Lt	Sub Lieutenant
UXB	Unexploded bomb
VAD	Voluntary Aid Detachment
WAAF	Women's Auxiliary Air force
WRAF	Women's Royal Air Force

1. *Before the War*

"The old inhabitants view with amazement the transformation scenes
enacted from day to day . . ."

Beckenham Times 1932

The years between the official ending of the First World War in 1919
and the outbreak of the Second World War in 1939 were momentous
ones for West Wickham. Gone was the Kentish village of 1,300 souls
living in rural tranquillity – in its place was a busy bustling town with
a population numbering around 20,000. Even Wickham's boundaries
had been altered in 1934 when, in the process of being transferred
from the jurisdiction of the Bromley Rural District Council to that of
the Beckenham Urban District Council, it lost some farmland to
Keston and gained a small part of the parish of Hayes.

The Avenue c 1930

1

Lime Tree Walk c 1935

Hawes Lane c 1935

2

The Lord of the Manor, Sir Stephen Lennard, had emigrated to Canada in 1929 after which his home, Wickham Court, became an hotel. The Rectory on Corkscrew Hill had been sold in 1925 to one Francis Chamberlain and renamed Glebe House. The little National School in School Road, unable to cope with the fast-rising Roll, closed in 1930, its pupils then being transferred to new Council Schools in Hawes Lane. Another Council School, Wickham Common School, opened in 1937.[1] Several private schools appeared on the scene.

The Parish Church of St. John the Baptist in Layhams Road had been augmented by two daughter churches – St. Francis of Assisi in Ravenswood Avenue and St. Mary of Nazareth in The Avenue. The tiny Congregational Chapel in North Road had succumbed to the pressure of events and a new, larger Congregational Church – Emmanuel – opened in 1929 in The Grove. Those of the Methodist, Baptist and Roman Catholic persuasions were similarly to be found in new purpose-built accommodation.

The High Street had been widened and older properties demolished or converted to accommodate modern shops. A Crown Post Office opened in 1933, provided in 1939 a seven day-a-week service: Sundays, Bank Holidays and Good Friday 9–10.30 am; and weekdays 8 am–7.30 pm. A Plaza Cinema opened next to the Post Office in 1933. Two more public houses opened – The Pickhurst Green Hotel in Pickhurst Lane and The Coney in Croydon Road – supplementing The Swan, The Wheatsheaf, The White Hart and The Railway Hotel. The clearing banks arrived in 1928.[2]

Transport facilities were much improved in 1921 when buses began running to and from West Wickham, and again in 1925 when the railway line was electrified. Mains drainage supplanted the cesspool system in 1928, putting one 'Stinky Harry', the driver of the collection cart, out of work.

Sports facilities were legion and included the use of glebe land bought as a memorial to the Revd. Bertie Roberts after his death in 1924.

Residents' Associations had sprung up. The West Wickham Residents Association had gone from strength to strength since its formation in 1929 and, according to its 1939 Year Book, had achieved a membership of 2,000. This Association, a lively body with many concerns, continued its campaign for roadside trees and was "happy to report that a number of roads have been planted this winter."

The Coney Hall & District Residents Association (CANDRA) was no less active and achieved national newspaper coverage in 1938 when, under the chairmanship of James Borders, it organised a mortgage strike among households on the Coney Hall estate, 400 of them taking part.

3

Wickham Court Hotel

(Under the same management as the Selsdon Park and Selsdon Court Hotels)

For less than is demanded by the most moderate London Hotel, you may obtain, only half an hour from the City and West End, the delights of the country as well as the last word in modern hotel service and equipment; in brief, these Hotels, with their own private 18-hole golf course (6,361 yards) in their own park of 230 acres, are unique.

Inclusive of full *en pension* (including afternoon tea), motor service between Hotel and East Croydon Station and Selsdon Park, golf (even at the week-end), swimming, dancing, use of billiard tables, tennis courts, squash rackets, electric gymnasium, putting courses, croquet lawn, children's sand beach and paddling pool, etc.

WEEKLY WINTER TERMS.
For one person—Single Room from 4½ to 5½ gns.
For one person—Double Room from 6 gns.
 With private bathroom from 8 gns.
For two persons—Double Room from 8 to 10 gns.
 With private bathroom from 10 to 13 gns.
Suites (comprising Large Double Room, Sitting Room and Bathroom) from 15½ to 17½ gns.

WEEKLY SUMMER TERMS.
For one person—Single Room from 6 to 7½ gns.
For one person—Double Room from 8 gns.
 With private bathroom from 10 gns.
For two persons—Double Room from 10 to 12 gns.
With private bathroom from 12½ to 16½ gns.
Private Suites from 20 to 22½ gns.

Allowances (must be claimed from Office in advance).

10/6 per week if not requiring lunch or tea Monday to Friday inclusive.

10/6 per week for children not requiring late dinner.

10/6 per week for nurses taking dinner in the Steward's room.

Pension allowance for temporary absence of not less than three days.

Residents on weekly terms give one week's notice, or accommodation will be charged.

Special menus can be provided at an additional charge.

Visitors' Servants, with board in Steward's Room: Winter Terms £3 3s. per week. Summer Terms £4 4s. per week.

Dogs are charged from 10s. 6d. per week, guests being responsible for any damage.

Corkage will be charged on all Alcoholics, Minerals, etc., brought into the Hotel.

MEALS (for non-residents).

Luncheon (inc. Coffee) 4/6 (Sunday 6/6).

Afternoon Tea 1/6 (Sunday 2/-).

Dinner (including Coffee) 6/6, Wednesday (including Dance) 7/6.

Permanent residents on Annual terms pay winter rates throughout the year.
Residents may partake of Meals in any Hotel without additional charge.
[The right to refuse food or accommodation without assigning any reasons is reserved.]

The following amenities are available to residents at all Hotels :

DANCING. Dancing takes place every Wednesday evening in the magnificent ballroom at Wickham Court, and every Saturday at Selsdon Park, residents at Wickham Court, Selsdon Park and Selsdon Court being equally welcome. The music is provided by leading London dance bands.

TENNIS. There are Grass and en-tout-cas Courts, set amidst ideal surroundings. Free to residents.

BILLIARDS. All Hotels have full-sized Championship Tables and Billiards is entirely free to residents.

AT SELSDON PARK :
OPEN-AIR BATHING POOL. Swimming in this large and well-equipped Pool is free to residents.
ELECTRIC GYMNASIUM free to residents.
SQUASH RACKETS. Championship Court by G. H. Carter, Ltd., entirely free to residents.
RIDING on the estate at very moderate charges.
BRIDGE. Bridge Parties are a regular evening feature of the Hotels.

Hawes Down School 1935

Wickham Common School 1937 *Pauline Terry*

Stocks Tree and Wickham House (converted to accommodate shops) *Alan de Maid*

The Coney 1985 *Joyce Walker*

The Swan and High Street 1936

But while God was in His Heaven, not all was right with the world. The machinations of Adolf Hitler's Nazi Germany were causing great unease, not just on the world scene, but at local level, with the threat of another war against Germany a real possibility. As early as 1935 the Baldwin Government had issued a circular on Air Raid Precautions. Two years later an ARP Act made local authorities responsible for ARP measures.

March 1938: Hitler takes over Austria and assures the world that he will make no further territorial claims in Europe and no intention of attacking Czechoslovakia.

The priest-in-charge of St. Mary of Nazareth, the Revd. H. K. Percival Smith, had initiated a Holiday Peace Movement in which French and German citizens were entertained every summer in West Wickham and the surrounding district. There was a feeling in some quarters in 1938 that in view of the international situation, German visitors should not be accorded hospitality. The Revd. Percival Smith disagreed and so 100 visitors arrived from France and Germany in July and August 1938, but even as they were being welcomed, preparations were going ahead for civil defence should the unthinkable come to pass.

Prospect Gardens, Wildacre

WEST WICKHAM. CORKSHREW HILL.

PHOTOCHROM COPYRIGHT
77999

"... preparations for ARP ... particularly good results achieved in West Wickham."

Beckenham Borough Council Minutes – January 1938

A speaker at a poorly attended Annual General Meeting of the West Wickham Constitutional Association in 1938, observed that the "people in the newly built areas like West Wickham did not take an interest in politics ... Their only interest seemed to be in foreign policy."[3] He believed that "at the bottom of young men's minds and the old men too, was the fear of war". Perhaps that speaker had read a report presented by the ARP Committee to the Beckenham Borough Council on the state of its preparations in which West Wickham was shown to be way ahead of other areas in the Borough. The ARP Committee expressed "its appreciation of the results obtained by the Head Warden of the West Wickham ARP area [H. M. Carter] which had been completed with 38 wardens, 12 assistant wardens and 13 male and 14 female First Aid personnel."[4] H. M. Carter, in an interview with a local newspaper reporter, spoke of one old gentleman offering his services based on the fact that he had fought in the Egyptian Campaign in the 1880s!

John Merigan, manager of the local Payantake store, was one of the first ARP volunteers in Beckenham and West Wickham – numbered 27 on the enrolment list. He was joined by solicitor Kenneth Wilkie and retired Ben Hughes. Another group was led by Francis Chamberlain; the Coney Hall group was led by John Chandler and his deputy Sydney Skipper. They trained two nights a week at Beckenham Fire Station in Bromley Road and were given anti-gas and general training and in liaison with the police and fire brigade. Eventually warden strength was increased so that every house in West Wickham was covered. One of the wardens' duties was to fit respirators and arrangements were made for 30,000 respirators to be stored in a depot at Hawes Down School.

There was some scepticism as to the efficacy of air raid precautions. The West Wickham branch of the Labour Party held a meeting in March 1938 at which the speaker gave voice to his convictions that "any future war would finish civilisation as we knew it. It was impossible to defend oneself against air raids except at tremendous cost . . ."[5] Members of the West Wickham branch of the Peace Pledge Union declined to participate "in preparations which they believe will hasten the destruction they are alleged to prevent."[6] Some individuals declared that in the event of a gas attack they would take to the Shirley Hills.

7 April   *Italy seizes Albania*

9

Part-time auxiliary firemen were recruited to supplement the Fire Brigades. The first members of the Beckenham Auxiliary Fire Service who signed on at the Old Council Chambers in Bromley Road in August 1938, included from West Wickham three members of the banking profession, Ron Pearce, Frank Preston and Ron Warner. They were typical of the recruits who were mainly professional men, even a professional artist, Kingsley Sutton. The part-time firemen underwent full training alongside the regular members of the Beckenham Brigade, in operating pumps, general firemanship and First Aid. One of the training officers was Oliver Woodman who was later to become Station Officer at West Wickham Fire Station.

The Red Cross Voluntary Aid Detachment, Kent 82, demobilised after the First World War, was re-formed in 1938 by Mrs. Margaret Caine, and its members soon became proficient in First Aid, Nursing and anti-gas techniques. The latter skills had been introduced into the training syllabus for it was assumed that poison gas would be used in the event of air attack.

September 1938 : Hitler seizes part of Czechoslovakia. A conference takes place between Neville Chamberlain, the British Prime Minister; Edouard Daladier, the French Prime Minister; Adolf Hitler; and the Italian leader, Benito Mussolini.

In September 1938 trenches were hurriedly dug at MacAndrew Playing Field and Blake Recreation Ground. At 4.30 pm on 26 September the Beckenham Borough Council received orders to immediately distribute respirators. At once the machinery of administration prepared by the ARP committee was put into operation and wardens were summoned to their respective posts that same evening. Three Beckenham firms, Burnham & Co., Perga Ltd. and Percy Jones (Twinlock) Ltd. whose workers had been prepared for the task of assembling respirators, were put to work. Lorries despatched the load from the three stores to fifteen distributing depots, including those at West Wickham: Justin Hall, Hawes Down School, Greenhayes School and the Coney Hall (now known as the Assembly Rooms). Some respirators, popularly called gas masks, were delivered that evening and the rest the following day.

The Munich crisis is resolved. Hitler gets everything he wants, including a large slice of Czechoslovakia. Neville Chamberlain returns from Munich having extracted a guarantee from Hitler that he will make no more territorial demands. Chamberlain claims that his conciliatory policy has brought 'peace with honour . . peace in our time.'

The West Wickham Left Book Club passed a resolution deploring the "National Government's shameful betrayal of Czechoslovakia, calling on the Government to stand firm with France . . against the threat of German Fascism."[7]

15 March 1939   Germany seizes the rest of Czechoslovakia.

There was an influx of Czech refugees into Britain, some arrived in West Wickham with more anticipated. A West Wickham Czech Refugee Fund came into existence.

April   Military Training Act conscripts men of 20 and 21 to six months compulsory military training.

By now the trenches so hurriedly dug the previous September had become derelict, but with war clouds growing darker they were quickly consolidated. Plans were approved for a shelter for 350 persons in MacAndrew Playing Field where an Anderson steel garden shelter was put on display. These steel shelters would be issued free to those compulsorily insured for National Health or those living on an annual income of £250 or less. Those with higher incomes were expected to provide themselves with shelters at their own expense. A survey was made of basements and cellars with a view to their being used as air raid shelters.

22 May   Germany and Italy become Allies

The Management Committee of the Lecture Hall in Sussex Road, having already agreed in 1937 to the Hall being earmarked as an ARP Post, gave permission for the Hall to be used by a mobile medical unit in the event of severe air raids. Public lectures were held there on Air Raid Precautions and included instruction in the preparation of refuge rooms in private houses. The ARP services were also in evidence during a mock air raid on 22 June. It had been intended that a squadron of Hurricanes would fly low over Beckenham and West Wickham and drop 262 mock bombs and that the Territorial Army's local Anti-Aircraft Battery would fire back equally inoffensively, but on the day heavy ground mist persisted at Biggin Hill aerodrome and the aerial part of the exercise was cancelled. 2,700 volunteers from Beckenham and West Wickham took part in the 'air raid', going into action when the warning sirens sounded at 8.07 am, manning Warden Posts, First Aid Depots and Ambulance Depots. Decontamination Squads stood by to sound rattles, giving warning of a gas attack. Rescue and Repair Squads also stood by. The Auxiliary Fire Service had 82 members on duty equipped with twelve Dennis trailer pumps. All the volunteers worked closely with 'P' Division of the Metropolitan Police and the main public utility undertakings.

11

West Wickham Fire Station was opened in Glebe Way in July 1939 with a siren on its tower and additional accommodation for nineteen trailer pumps. Land at Burroughs Wellcome at Park Langley was used for the storage of more pumps. Steps were then taken to obtain towing vehicles for the pumps. Some were donated, others were bought, including three Rolls-Royces and a Buick that had been used for filming in the desert. (The latter vehicle was quickly appropriated for use as a staff car, but it was to come to an inglorious end in an incident at Park Langley.) The interiors of the cars were ripped out, shelves and racks put up for storage of hoses and other items of equipment, and tow bars affixed. Later on Auxiliary Towing Vehicles were supplied.

Buick – "an inglorious end"   *Oliver Woodman*

On 1 September a sub Station was opened in the Coney Hall. The Toc H premises adjacent to the Rectory were used for the vehicles while the cow-sheds and barns served as sleeping quarters. This sub Station was manned by AFS personnel 24 hours a day. One of those drafted into the AFS was Bob Smith, a lorry driver employed by Messrs Ray whose lorry it was that was requisitioned as a towing vehicle! The pond close to the Coney Hall was used for training purposes.

'Action Stations' were established at 61 Sherwood Way, Wickham Park Sports Club (where a Ford V8 served as the towing vehicle), 118 Copse Avenue, 31 Pine Avenue, Sandiland Crescent, Birch Tree Avenue and at the Fire Station. These Action Stations were manned by members of the AFS from 8 pm to 8 am.

Watch Room at the Coney Hall

Despite the difficult and worrying times, the social calendar was adhered to much as usual. The West Wickham Fair and Flitch attracted large crowds to Sparrows Den. A new church bell, christened 'Elizabeth', was dedicated at St. John's Church by the Bishop of Croydon. The Revd. Percival Smith and twelve local people visited Germany at the invitation of those who had enjoyed Wickham hospitality in 1938. The Flower Show was held in Justin Hall.

The Civil Defence Services took another opportunity to perfect their skills when the whole of Kent was 'blacked-out' on 9 August from 12.30 am to 4 am. Those taking part in West Wickham were an ambulance section with stretcher parties, based at Hawes Down Infants School; First Aiders on duty at the Hawes Down Clinic, transformed into a Casualty Clearing Station; other First Aiders were on duty at an Aid Post in Wickham Common School.

Gates Green Road 1936

24 August   *Emergency Powers Defence Act passed. Military Reservists called up.*

The Warren in Croydon Road, home of a Metropolitan Police Sports Club, stored quantities of cardboard coffins in expectation of heavy civilian casualties and beds were moved into the Club House in readiness for police casualties.

In Beckenham a branch was formed of the Women's Voluntary Service for Civil Defence purposes. Office accommodation was provided in the Old Council Chambers in Bromley Road, together with paid clerical assistance. The ladies were soon in action appealing for clothes for victims of possible air raids. Within three months the WVS had opened five canteens at Aid Posts and Warden Posts, one of which was at the Hawes Down School.

Provision was made for animals who might be injured in air raids, at a veterinary surgery in Croydon Road, Beckenham. Owners were advised to send their pets into the country or else have them put down. Many owners took the latter advice and the Dog Shop at 63 High Street was busy, tragically busy.

The schools had not been unaffected by the threat of war. Various members of staff who belonged to the Territorial Army went on prolonged summer training camps. A classroom in Hawes Down School was requisitioned for ARP work, and Wickham Common School, as well as hosting an Aid Post, had a Warden Post in the boiler-room where Herbert Killick was Post Warden. This particular Post was known as the Do-Duck Inn because of the low headroom at its entrance. No plans had been made for the evacuation of children because West Wickham was in a 'neutral' area, i.e. not to be evacuated and not to be used for reception purposes.

Friday 1 September 1939 was a glorious hot summer's day. Miss Mercia Sansom was on the staff of Wickham Common Primary School "and in common with most primary teachers of the day had a class of over 50 children. We tried to carry on as if it were an ordinary school day, but as we were having mid-morning milk the headmaster, who had brought his own portable radio to school with him, came out to us as we were sitting on the grass and said 'Send the children home, Germany has invaded Poland!' "[8] Later that day schools were officially instructed not to open on 4 September because of the worsening international situation.

ARP services had been summoned for duty on the evening of 31 August. The following day saw increased activity in all directions – sandbags were filled and placed around buildings and a black-out of streets and houses came into operation as dusk fell. By Saturday 2 September all the ARP services were in a state of readiness.

Britain sends an ultimatum to Germany demanding that she withdraw her forces from Poland. When this is refused the Prime Minister addresses the British nation on the wireless on 3 September at 11.15 am.

"I am speaking to you from the Cabinet Room at 10 Downing Street. This morning the British Ambassador in Berlin handed the German Government a final note stating that unless we heard from them by 11 o'clock that they were prepared at once to withdraw their troops from Poland, a state of war would exist between us. I have to tell you that no such undertaking has been received, and that consequently this country is at war with Germany."

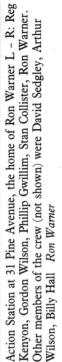

Action Station at 31 Pine Avenue, the home of Ron Warner L – R: Reg Kenyon, Gordon Wilson, Phillip Gwillim, Stan Collister, Ron Warner. Other members of the crew (not shown) were David Sedgley, Arthur Wilson, Billy Hall *Ron Warner*

Some crew members of the Action Station at Wickham Park Sports Club. Back row L – R: Les Crisp, Clive Housden, Ernie Altoff, Frank Preston, Alan Adams. Front row L – R: Arthur Brown, Len Tully *Frank Preston*

2. *September – December 1939*

"The Memorial . . . stood like a sentinel . . . and awaited the next generation – the world was in turmoil once more."

West Wickham and the Great War

Within a few minutes of the end of Neville Chamberlain's fateful speech the sirens sounded, giving warning of an air raid. It was a Sunday morning and many people were attending church services. In St. Francis Church where Choral Eucharist had been celebrated, the adults remained in their seats as the choir boys were sent down to the stoke-hole beneath the church. The service at St. John's was brought to a close and the congregation dispersed, as did those attending the Emmanuel and Methodist Churches. Afterwards the rector at St. John's discovered that the cellar was being used as a public air raid shelter.

Those at home reacted in different ways. Some came out of their homes and gazed skywards, but most made ready their refuge rooms by pinning up blankets at windows in readiness for the expected gas attack. Others filled their baths with water, as advised by the authorities. Fortunately the alert was a false alarm and the 'All Clear' was soon sounded.

One couple responded very positively. On that first day of war, Norman Faulkner, a chartered accountant from Langley Way, married Joan Bowyer by special licence in St. John's Church.

All cinemas and theatres were closed down, thus denying the patrons of the Odeon Cinema (formerly the Plaza) in Station Road, the pleasure of watching Will Hay in 'Ask a Policeman'.

An appeal was made by the Matron of the Children's Heart Hospital in Woodland Way for volunteers to fill the 30,000 sandbags necessary to protect the building. Her appeal was answered by local firemen who delighted the children with their visits. The Coney Hill Home for Crippled Children in Croydon Road was also afforded assistance by the firemen. It did help having a member of the AFS as its head gardener – Bertie Fordham.

Members of CANDRA dug trenches in Birch Tree Avenue. Ken Nottle, the Group Scoutmaster of the 1st West Wickham Troop,

17

announced that he would "be glad to hear from boys who are prepared to help with ARP messages etc."[9] The Peace Pledge Union stated that "some members volunteered for stretcher work service" and "that pacifists would do their utmost to stem any flood of hate that was likely to arise between the peoples of Britain and Germany."[10] The West Wickham Women's Constitutional Association responded to the situation by suspending all political activities, and forming a working party to make clothes for children and soldiers. The hostilities between the mortgage strikers in Coney Hall and the bailiffs were called to a temporary halt, for as a result of the Courts Emergency Powers Act being rushed through Parliament, building societies could no longer execute orders for the possession of houses without leave of the court. This did away with the need in Coney Hall for bailiff-chasers and pickets. The Wickham Park Sports Club curtailed its activities, but the West Wickham Football Club and the Bowling Club stated their intentions of carrying on as usual. The rector of St. John's Church hurried home from holiday in Belgium to supervise an unusual interment, that of the burying of the medieval glass windows in special chests, by J & R Killick Ltd.

War also brought about a drastic reduction in trade for local businesses, and residents were exhorted to shop locally.

Both Council and private schools had been closed. One of the first of the private schools to re-open on 20 September was St. David's College "in the safety zone between West Wickham and Beckenham with full ARP in spacious grounds."[11] The full ARP in spacious grounds – a shelter erected in a field – was invariably filled with water (a story often repeated in Wickham in days to come), and so the original schoolroom in 29 South Eden Park Road was strengthened to become an additional shelter. There had been a proposal by a few parents to move the children to the country and to found a boarding school, but nothing came of this suggestion. Some parents made their own arrangements with the result that St. David's Roll fell dramatically, but the College survived by the expedient of "accepting students of all ages who, for whatever reason, needed to maintain their studies."[12] 'All ages' ranged from 3–33!

Wickham College in Station Road also re-opened in September after a shelter was constructed in what was thought to be the remains of an old tunnel beneath the building. Legend had it that the cellar was the blocked-up remains of a passage to the former manor house, Wickham Court, in Layhams Road. (The enquiring mind might ask how the tunnel could negotiate the steep hill between the College and Wickham Court.)

Another school was opened in St. Mary's Church Hall for forty

Wickham girls attending school in Croydon, Sydenham and Lewisham, whose schools had been evacuated but with no provision made for those whose homes were outside the boroughs concerned.

Medieval glass in St. John the Baptist Church *Joyce Walker*

Although the Council Schools remained closed, a home tuition scheme in English, Arithmetic and Current Events was introduced in which small groups of children met in private houses where they were taught by teachers from their own schools. Mrs. Dorothy Wingent, then living at 84 Manor Park Road, played hostess to one group and enjoyed the experience enormously. By the end of October 283

19

children from Hawes Down Junior School were being taught in this fashion.

The teachers "were made very welcome. It gave an opportunity for more individual attention, the children seemed to enjoy it and . . . [we] became used to going around the different houses."[13]

Mercia Sansom remembers that period too, when "staff had to carry all the books and materials needed from house to house – mostly on bicycles . . . This went on right through the winter and I have vivid memories of cycling round the Coney Hall estate in the snow, shedding reading books and pencils as I skidded round the corners. The authorities finally decided to build shelters at the school and tunnelled into the high banks at the back of the playground so that we could go in at ground level."[14]

Wickham Common School 1990 showing the banks once used as air raid shelters *Joyce Walker*

The Hawes Down Schools re-opened on 4 December after some shelters had been built. Hawes Down Junior School with a roll of 175 used the Infants' School premises from 8.30 am until 12 noon. The Senior School made use of the same premises from 12.30 pm until 4 pm. There were then, still a number of staff and pupils working in private houses. The infants themselves were hostages to fortune. The five-year-olds remained at home; some of the six-year-olds attended Springfield in Springfield Gardens with the remainder

20

attending their own school, as did the seven-year-olds. At Springfield two downstairs rooms, with walls approximately fourteen inches thick, were used as classrooms for 50 children. A third room was strengthened to provide a shelter for the children.

At Wickham Common School, after trenches had been constructed, some of the junior pupils were able to resume their education, albeit on a part-time basis, sharing their premises with pupils from Balgowan School. The Beckenham pupils travelled to Wickham Common School, most by train to Hayes, walking the rest of the way to begin their half-day at 8.30 am.

29 September   *National Registration Identity Cards issued.*
September–October   *Ministry of National Service extends call-up for men aged between 27 and 41 years of age.*

In October a tribunal was established at Bromley to consider the circumstances of enemy aliens living in the area. Many of those who came before the tribunal did so for purely technical reasons as in the case of the Czech and Austrian refugees. It was not realised at the time that the fledgling Coney Hill Baptist Church would become enmeshed in the dealings of the tribunal.

Coney Hill Road 1936

When the War began the ARP organisations and the Fire Brigades were in a high state of readiness. They were backed up by voluntary organisations, among them two Voluntary Aid Detachments of the British Red Cross Society – Kent 82 and Kent 39, the latter a men's detachment based in Beckenham, formed out of the Rover Crew of the 3rd West Wickham Scout Group; and later on in the War, Kent 234, a ladies' detachment based in Coney Hall and led by Mrs. Florence Quaif. Not in uniform but just as effective were those members of the Women's Institute who helped in the canteen at West Wickham Fire Station.

One of the members of Kent 39 was George Raymond who, acting on standing orders, reported on 3 September 1939 to the Churchfields Road Depot in Beckenham. In the early days no proper sleeping accommodation was provided, so the dustcarts there were pressed into service! Accommodation was also a problem at West Wickham Fire Station. Houses had been built nearby to accommodate the pre-war complement of regular firemen, but with the creation of AFS Action Stations, the problem became acute. This situation was eased somewhat when flats over the shops in Glebe Way were requisitioned for sleeping quarters. Fortunately most were empty or else being used to store newsprint for Fleet Street. The AFS organised a canteen in one of the flats and working hours became much more tenable.

The Fire Service collated information on the whereabouts of local ponds for use in time of emergency. Static Emergency Water Supply Tanks holding 5,000 gallons of water appeared in various places. There was one where West Wickham Library now stands, and another in MacAndrew Playing Field. Road works on the new Glebe Way had been abandoned on the outbreak of hostilities, and the twenty-feet-deep cutting made through the brow of the hill by the contractors began to fill with spring water, thus forming a large lake. It stretched from the gate into the cricket field to what is now Glebe Court.[15] Firemen stopped up the ends and "we had thousands upon thousands of gallons of water."[16] Among ponds earmarked for use was the one in Croydon Road adjacent and to the rear of what is now Payless Stores; the pond in Bramley Way was also noted.

On the outbreak of war the civil ambulance service, which up to that time had been staffed and administered by the Fire Brigade, was transferred to the Medical Officer of Health, and the staff were then drawn from the ARP Medical Services. The Civil Defence Services were ready, but for what and when? The waiting period had begun.

Meanwhile those who were not prepared to join the Armed Forces appeared before tribunals. They were given the alternatives of agricultural work, forestry or joining the Merchant Navy. Others were directed to the ARP Service.

December   *Places of public entertainment are re-opened. The land war in France is a stalemate.*

A few days before Christmas the War Memorial which had been moved from the High Street to a more peaceful location on Corkscrew Hill, was re-dedicated by the Bishop of Croydon. " . . . The Memorial now stood like a sentinel . . . and awaited the next generation. . . "[17]

Despite the War, Christmas was celebrated as usual at the Children's Heart Hospital; the Aberdare Memorial Home for Boys, also in Woodland Way and where every boy was given a shiny new shilling; and at the Coney Hill Children's Home. The new CANDRA Social Club opened in premises over the Temple Motors Garage (now Payless Stores) with a party on Boxing Day. A few days later came the official opening with 500 guests present, who danced to the music of CANDRA's own band. A Christmas party was organised for full-time personnel of the Hawes Down ARP Centre. There were joyous celebrations on Christmas Day at the new Maternity Home in Stone Park Avenue in Beckenham with the arrival of the first baby to be born there – a daughter for Mrs. Elsie Smith of Langley Way. The Mayor of Beckenham was sufficiently moved to mark the occasion with the presentation of a silver cup.

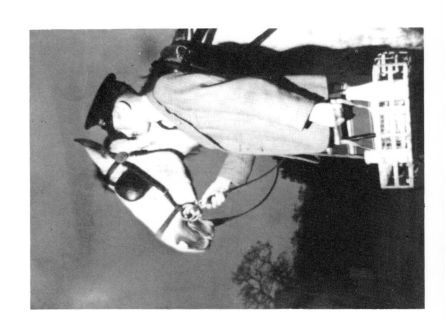

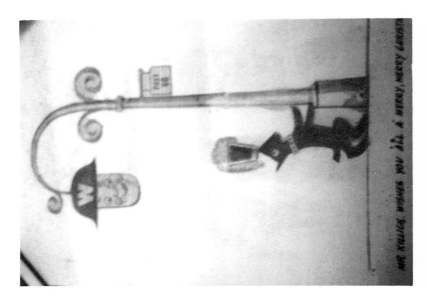

24

3. *1940*

"Man Anti-Tank Line . . . Man line bombing pits at road blocks . . . Insert Anti-Tank Rails . . . Glebe House . . . Corkscrew Hill . . ."

> Extracts from Invasion Orders to 'A' Company 55 Kent Bn Home Guard

8 January   *Food rationing introduced – bacon, ham, butter and sugar*

Early in 1940 there was a 'Grow More Food' campaign. Lawns were dug up and given over to vegetables. Public land was turned over to allotments – two acres of MacAndrew Flower Gardens; 93 plots on the Coney Hall Recreation Ground where a plough from Layhams Farm was used to dig over the ground. Four acres of the Langley Park Golf Course were ploughed up, planted with potatoes and designated 'Ground under repair'. However the golfers' sacrifice was mostly in vain for when the potatoes were harvested they were declared unfit for human consumption and sold as pig food.

Other allotments appeared in Grosvenor Road, Pickhurst Rise, Oak Lodge, Pine Avenue, Lime Tree Walk, Blake Recreation Ground, Coney Hill Road, Springfield, The Alders, Manor Road and Hawes Lane. Part of Wickham Park Sports Club fell to the 'plotters', as the allotment holders were known. The plotters on the latter territory had the added advantage of being club members and therefore had access to the bar.

There were allotments in Glebe Way cultivated by firemen, the resulting produce considerably enhancing the canteen menu. The firemen also reared chickens on a plot adjoining the fish restaurant, and rabbits in the backyards of other shops in Glebe Way.

(opposite, left)   'Do-Duck Inn' Christmas card   *Doreen Meloy*

(opposite, right)   Ted Becket and 'Sam'. Ted Becket became a War Reserve policeman before joining the Army   *Sarah Becket*

At the Fire Station where a duck was kept in a hutch, duck eggs appeared on the canteen menu. Satisfied customers decided to treat the duck to a swim in the five feet deep pumping pit (she never having had her feet wet) but she repaid the compliment by ceasing to lay any more eggs.

Summer-time begins on 25 February

Full-time schooling was resumed for the senior department of Hawes Down School on 11 March when the main building was brought back into use – the juniors remained part-time for a few more weeks. Air Raid drill was practised in the new trenches. Wickham Common School resumed full-time schooling after its guests from Balgowan School were able to return to their own premises.

The first of the Red Cross Working Parties was organised by Florence Quaif in her home at 66 Chestnut Avenue, out of which grew the West Wickham Hospital Supply & Services Fund. The first consignment of gifts consisting of socks, operation stockings, shirts and night-shirts, was blessed on its way by the Revd. C. A. Shaw Page. Other Working Parties were established at 124 Chestnut Avenue, the small Lecture Hall, 69 Gates Green Road, St. Mary's Church Hall and Emmanuel Church Hall. All the Working Parties were linked to the Bromley Clearing House.

Glebe House was the home of a fourteen-bedded American Hospital for use in time of emergency. It was so-called because all the equipment was supplied by the American Red Cross. The local Voluntary Aid Detachment, Kent 82, regularly checked the equipment and its members were on permanent stand-by. Other exigencies of war required that staff at the Library at 83 Station Road exchanged and issued gas masks as well as books!

The RSPCA put up a notice outside the West Wickham Riding School in Links Road – 'Animals Air Raid Shelter'. Many traders still used a horse and cart for delivery purposes.

March   *Meat rationed*

The West Wickham Citizens Advice Bureau was opened in March in temporary accommodation in the Lecture Hall. Later it set up shop in Emmanuel Church Hall. There was another opening of a different kind, that of the Coney Hill Baptist Church where the Revd. A. J. Garnier, a retired Baptist Missionary, was inducted as its first Minister. Another important event in Coney Hall was the formation of the Coney Hall Trust, its trustees responsible for the Coney Hall for the benefit of the neighbourhood. The ladies of the West Wickham

26

Women's Institute were not to be outdone and celebrated the Institute's 21st birthday in some style. Lady Lennard marked the occasion with the presentation of a silver trophy. Another 21st birthday celebrated was that of the West Wickham Girls' Club.

Brownies, Girl Guides, Wolf Cubs and Boy Scouts were well represented in West Wickham and they applied themselves to the needs of the war effort, particularly when appeals for salvage were made. The Scouts in particular regularly collected old newspapers, using the Girl Guide Hut in Woodland Way as a depot.

Servicemen, never far from people's thoughts, were at the forefront of one of West Wickham Residents Association's schemes to raise funds for the regular despatch of comforts to local men. It was because so many young men were in the Armed Forces that the Coney Hall Football Club was having difficulty in raising a team. The West Wickham Football Club struggled to field two teams.

9 April   *Germany invades Norway and Denmark*

The West Wickham Fair and Flitch was held in Sparrows Den over the Whitsun Holiday. Attendances were down on the Bank Holiday Monday, the day having been declared a normal working day. Nevertheless the 'Trial by Jury for the Wickham Flitch held in the Court of Married Happiness' went ahead, produced by the West Wickham Dramatic Society.

The cricketers of both Wickham Park Sports Club and West Wickham Cricket Club fulfilled their fixtures. On 5 May a cricket match in aid of Red Cross funds was staged on WWCC's ground, against a London Counties team which included Leslie Todd the Kent cricketer. There were no county championships or international matches, but first-class players, subject to the demands of military service, were able to display their skills in such teams as the London Counties and British Empire teams, both touring sides. Equally crowd-pulling was the match between West Wickham and the Bowling Club. Charles Couchman did his best to remain an impartial umpire.

9 May   *First bomb on British mainland (near Canterbury)*
10 May   *Germany invades France and the Low Countries. Neville Chamberlain resigns as Prime Minister and is succeeded by Winston Churchill.*

On 14 May the Secretary of State for War, Anthony Eden, appealed on the radio for civilians to come forward to create a force of Local Defence Volunteers. Within a week 250,000 men had joined and a million by August, overwhelming the local authorities, not least at local police stations where the volunteers had been told to report.

There is certainly the right camp atmosphere in this gathering of the Girl Guides from Beckenham, Penge, Anerley and West Wickham at "Heartsease," West Wickham.

Girl Guides at Heartsease 1942 *Croydon Advertiser*

Whit Monday, May 13th   11 a.m.

IN THE LARGE MARQUEE

TRIAL BY JURY for the WICKHAM FLITCH

Held in the Court of Married Happiness

Produced by

THE WEST WICKHAM DRAMATIC SOCIETY

(Wickham is staging the only Flitch Trial of the year)

The Committee's appreciative thanks to J. Clayton Taylor, Esq: for presenting THE FLITCH for yet another year.

Judge: F. D. L. BURGE

Clerk to the Court: A. H. TAMMADGE

Counsel for the Flitch: PATRICK MORIARTY

Case No. 1.

Mr. & Mrs. S. W. QUAIF v. THE FLITCH
Counsel for the Claimants: ALBERT WESTLEY

Case No. 2.

Mr. & Mrs. "ERSATZ" v. THE FLITCH
(Leonard Tully and Dorothy Pester)
Counsel for Claimants: EDWARD HOLLAND

Case No. 3.

Mr. & Mrs. G. M. SYER v. THE FLITCH
Counsel for Claimants: RITA YATES

Foreman of the Jury: H. CHESWICK

TICKETS: 2/6 1/6 1/-

A Flitch Trial offers ideal entertainment for Bank Holiday morning: What better link with Old England? If you are attending your first Flitch Trial - a real treat awaits you.

ACCIDENTS— should be reported to the Staff of the First Aid Posts—without delay!

West Wickham Fair and Flitch

Under the Auspices of West Wickham (Kent) Community Council)

— IN AID OF LOCAL CHARITIES —
— AND HOSPITALS —

Sparrow's Den
Corkscrew Hill
(By kind permission of Beckenham Borough Council)

WHITSUN
SATURDAY
& MONDAY
MAY 11th & 13th

Souvenir Programme

1940

Don't Overlook Inside Cover

PRICE 2d.

29

Arthur Davie of Boleyn Gardens tried to sign on that first day at Bromley Police Station, but it was under siege from would-be LDVs. Eventually he was told to report to Springfield in Springfield Gardens where at last his name was taken along with those of many other local men. A headquarters was set up in what is now Kathleen Moore Court in Woodland Way. Because of his service as a World War One soldier, Arthur Davie was appointed Lieutenant of 3 Platoon 'A' Company of P.5,[18] which set up its own headquarters at 31 Corkscrew Hill. Initially its armoury consisted of five rifles which were kept chained up in Greenhayes School, the key being held by Lt. Davie. 'B' Company set up headquarters in Coney Hill Road.

Bob Squires was a member of the LDV for a short while. When Lee Enfield rifles became available he was sent to collect a supply from Bromley. The memory of having to degrease the rifles, dressed in a formal suit, is not a happy one for him.

As more equipment arrived and training progressed, so the defences became more elaborate – Browning automatic rifles, Thompson sub-machine guns and the Northover Projector. This latter piece of equipment resembled a drainpipe mounted on two legs. It was designed to discharge glass bottles containing a phosphorous mixture which burst into vivid flames, giving off quantities of suffocating smoke upon exposure to air. Wickham Park Sports Club served as a training ground for grenade throwing. The former Village Church opposite The Wheatsheaf was used for drill and instructional purposes.

Belgian and Dutch refugees arrived in the district in May, a large camp having been established in Hayes as a clearing centre. 200

Some members of 'B' Company 55 Kent Bn Home Guard *Ivy Crier*

homes were offered to the refugees in West Wickham where a staff of voluntary workers answered enquiries in Emmanuel Church Hall.

26 May – 4 June   *Evacuation of the BEF and Allied soldiers from Dunkirk. Hundreds of large and small ships succeed in rescuing 333,000 troops before Dunkirk falls.*

By now the number of public air raid shelters in Wickham had been increased and were regularly publicised in local newspapers. They were:

		Accommodation
Trench Shelters:	MacAndrew Playing Field	450
	Blake Recreation Ground	300
	Coney Hall Recreation Ground	300
Shop Shelter:	Wheatsheaf Parade	75
Surface Shelter:	Yew Tree Cottage	100

10 June   *Italy enters the War on the German side.*

In the midst of all these activities the Coney Hill Baptist Church was deprived of its minister, the Revd. A. J. Garnier. An Italian by birth, he was given just 30 minutes notice before being taken away for internment on the Isle of Man as an enemy alien. Mr. Garnier's wife, British by birth as were their three children, accepted an invitation to continue her husband's ministry while the church authorities made strenuous efforts to obtain his release. The Minister, having laboured for 33 years as a missionary in China, had never been in England long enough to qualify for naturalisation. The Revd. Garnier's flock was able to welcome his return a few months later in August.

18 June   *Churchill warns that "the whole might and fury of the enemy must very soon be turned on us." The first bombs in the London area fall on ploughland in nearby Addington.*
22 June   *France signs an armistice with Germany. Britain is now alone and Hitler's next target. Air superiority is essential. So begins the Battle for Britain.*

The so-called 'phoney war' had lulled the population into a false sense of security, but with the fall of France and bombs being dropped on Britain, some of those without air raid shelters were galvanised into action. Typical at this time were the Wingent and Smith and Land families who joined forces and had an underground shelter built in the back garden of 86 Manor Park Road the home of Harold Smith. It was to prove a wise decision.

31

Invasion orders to 'A' Company 3 Platoon 55 Kent Bn Home Guard
Arthur Davie

Anti-Tank block adjacent to Hawes Down Infants School
Joyce Walker

As the battle for air superiority raged overhead, preparations for resistance to an invasion were intensified with the LDV Force (renamed the Home Guard) well to the fore. The defences in West Wickham were part of the outer line of defence around London – anti-tank lines with deep trenches, barriers, pillboxes and road blocks. At the time it was expected that these lines would be held to the last man – there would be no withdrawal. Lieutenant Davie's Company was split – some were posted to trenches dug around the Metropolitan Police Radio Station at Keston, while others manned fire trenches by the tank traps at the bottom of Corkscrew Hill and in Stambourne Way at its junction with Wickham Court Road. The obstacles at Corkscrew Hill consisted of concrete blocks with holes bored through their centres, and on the given command, steel pipes would be threaded through the blocks and so bar Corkscrew Hill to the invaders. Similar concrete blocks were erected at the junction of Hawes Lane and Silver Lane and sited just inside the school grounds there and in the front garden of 128 Hawes Lane. Seven feet deep trenches were dug all the way down Corkscrew Hill by the Home Guard.

Road signs were taken down so as to hinder the enemy. The bells of St. John's and St. Francis' angelus bell fell silent, to be rung only as a warning of invasion. Poles were erected in Sparrows Den to deter enemy parachutists. Houses in Wood Lodge Lane backing on to Addington Bottom had concrete blocks positioned between them so that tanks would be unable to advance through them. Other blocks were positioned in strategic positions, including Driv Lane (Woodland Way at its junction with Oaklands Avenue). The bank on the Common side of Croydon Road between Pole Cat Alley and Prestons Road was mined with drums of sump oil and creosote to hold up the invaders. Deep tank traps were dug across school playing fields and parkland, and right through Spring Park Woods. One anti-tank ditch was set to go across West Wickham Football Club's pitch but Colonel (as he was by then) F. W. Chamberlain was able to have it diverted through the grounds of Glebe House behind the Club's pavilion. A pillbox was erected in the front garden of 31 Corkscrew Hill and a blockhouse in the garden of No. 42 on the other side of the road. There was another pillbox, albeit a rather unorthodox one, in a corner of St. John's churchyard near the lychgate. It was a very large hollow tree capable of accommodating five or six men who would have a commanding view of the cross-roads.

Stocks of food were stored in 'shadow larders' which, in the event of an invasion, would have allowed a distribution of about 9lbs a head of tinned meat, soup, stew or beans, tinned milk, emergency biscuits, sugar, margarine and tea. Florence Quaif, organiser of 'Green' area

(Coney Hall), supervised the distribution of supplies to 44 local food-minders who gave over part of their houses for the purpose. These ladies would distribute, if necessary, the supplies to the 200 or so householders for whom they were each responsible.

Among Florence Quaif's helpers were Mrs. Ada James and Mrs. Brooks, both of Chestnut Avenue, and Mrs. Fitt. "Three of us in the WVS had to go round every house inside the tank trap across Corkscrew Hill and if there had been an invasion we would have been closed off, so we had to be completely self-supporting. Mrs. Leslie had sacks of flour and I here, had a cache of food and put it all round the sitting-room window covered with a rather nice velvet bedspread . . . We literally spent hours and hours and got it all worked out – the whole of this area – working through the night – wrote slips out, notified everybody . . . if there was trouble they had to come here . . .''[19]

"Prime Minister to Home Secretary: The police and as soon as possible the ARP services are to be divided into combatant and non-combatant, armed and unarmed. The armed will co-operate actively in fighting with the Home Guard and regulars in their neighbourhood.''[20]

The ARP services in Wickham were given a general instruction to use guns taken from German soldiers, having had previous instruction in the use of Lee Enfield rifles. The Civil Defence moved into a higher gear in expectation of severe air raids. Individual households banded together for mutual support. Residents in Langley Way formed an organisation of fire parties and aid parties known as the Langley Way Home Security Council. A charge of 5/- per house was levied, which with a monthly payment of 6d., enabled a purchase to be made of 40 stirrup pumps. Other ARP Street Associations were formed in Pickhurst Rise, Wickham Chase and Goodhart Way.

4 July   *Italians cross Sudan border*

It was an exciting time for children with all these preparations going on around them. School routine was disrupted but not always to the children's liking. The summer term ended, but schools remained open for attendance on a voluntary basis with the staff staggering their fourteen days leave. The response was not very good.

The Government set up an Overseas Evacuation Scheme and offered free passages for children, to Canada and the USA. Several parents in Beckenham and West Wickham took advantage of the scheme with the first contingent arriving safely in Canada in August. The second contingent was not so fortunate. The son and daughter of Mr. and

Mrs. Poupard were on the *Volendam* when it was torpedoed and badly holed on 30 August, 70 miles off Bloody Foreland. A second torpedo failed to explode. The ship's captain succeeded in transferring his passengers by lifeboats to other ships in the convoy and the young Poupards survived, none the worse for their ordeal. Probably Mercia Sansom was part of this episode. "One day I shall never forget was the one I was told to take four children to Euston en route for Canada. They were children I did not know, two sets of twins, a boy and a girl in each family, one about ten, the other fourteen – and each carrying just their own hand luggage and the ubiquitous gas mask. The worst moment was parting them from their parents at West Wickham Station. At Charing Cross I managed to get a taxi to Euston. I had not been told that each child had been provided with a carton of milk for the journey. One boy leaned back in the taxi on his haversack and burst his carton of milk. I was soon aware that a trail of milk was following us everywhere. At Euston Station I got hold of a friendly waitress who lent me a tray and I unpacked the boy's haversack and had to wring the milk out of his pyjamas! I saw the children on a train for Liverpool where they stayed overnight at a hostel which was damaged by an incendiary bomb during the night. Then a day or two later the news broke that their ship had been torpedoed. It was some heart-aching days before I learned that all four children had been rescued – the two girls by one ship and the two boys by another. The father of the older children came to me and said, 'I will never part from my children again'." [21]

Mercia Sansom undertook other escorts, sometimes in the company of Alan Nelson, also a teacher at Wickham Common School. One boy from the school was escorted by them en route for the USA. "We went along to receive this boy and his luggage . . . The father opened the door . . . his face absolutely red and swollen with suppressed emotions . . . as he parted with his son." [22] Other children from West Wickham travelled to Canada privately, having made contacts through a pen-pal scheme in existence at Hawes Down School.

News of servicemen missing in France filtered through. Corporal Gerald Parsons of Ravenswood Avenue, missing since May, was reported a prisoner-of-war, as was Major Leslie Lauste, a doctor attached to a hospital in Boulogne. He too lived in Ravenswood Avenue. There was no news of Lieutenant John Stephenson of Sherwood Way.

The Government appeals to the Youth Services to meet the needs of the 14–18 year olds who have left school, especially those awaiting call-up and who are unattached to any youth organisation.

Südost

Die Parkanlagen des Südostens sind kleiner als die der anderen Bereiche. Zwischen Greenwich und Bromley schiebt sich von Osten her eine offenere und weniger stark bebaute Zone ein. Sie ist durch große Schaffarmen gekennzeichnet.

Durch die Sternwarte von Greenwich ist der Meridian $0°$ westöstlicher Länge festgelegt. In Greenwich befindet sich das Marinemuseum.

Wehrwichtige Anlagen

Stadtteil	Kr.	G.W.	El.W.	W.W.	Ka.	Bemerkungen
Beckenham	1		1			
Bellingham		1				
Bromley	1	1				
Camberwell	1					
Deptford		1				
Dulwich	4					
East Wickham . .						Ballonsperre
Elmers End		1				
Eltham	1					
Greenwich				1		
Grove Park	1					
Hither Green . . .	1					
Lee Green	1					
Lewisham	2					
Lower Sydenham		1				
New Beckenham	1					
Nunhead				1		
Peckham	1	1				
Plaistow.	1					
Plumstead			1			
Shooter's Hill . .	5					
Sidcup.	2					
West Wickham. .	1					

Kr. = Krankenhaus; G. W. = Gaswerk; El. W. = Elektrizitätswerk; W. W. = Wasserwerk; Ka. = Kaserne.

Wehrwichtig sind außerdem: das Marineinstitut (Greenwich); die Militärakademie (Woolwich) mit Militärärztlicher Akademie, Militärkrankenhäusern, Artilleriekasernen; Cambridge Kasernen, Schieß- und Exerzierplätze, Waffenlager.

Warengroßlager sind im Südosten zahlreich (z. B. für Tee, Kakao, Kaffee).

Die **Industrie** beschränkt sich auf eine Motorradfabrik und zwei Zünderfabriken, die Herstellung geodätischer Instrumente (in Camberwell) und eine Fabrik für Induktionsbrücken und andere elektrische Geräte.

36

An Army Cadet Corps was formed in Coney Hall, commanded by Lieutenant-Colonel C. A. Shaw Page. The Corps was based in the Coney Hall where the inaugural speech was given by George Allison, then manager of Arsenal Football Club.

10 July	*A nationwide appeal goes out for aluminium – pots and pans, tubes of vacuum cleaners, ornaments and even thimbles – to be donated to the war effort.*
22 July	*Tea, margarine and cooking fats rationed. Free or cheap milk is available to mothers.*
4 August	*Italians invade British Somaliland.*

King George VI visited West Wickham on 10 August when 4,000 members of the Home Guard paraded on West Wickham Cricket Club's ground. Many of those present, "an assorted and untried body of civilians with somewhere in the region of one week's notice, but how we drilled and perspired that week."[23] Uniforms were hastily collected from the Old Public Halls in Beckenham, "trousers in one corner, blouses in another, caps in a third . . . what a thrill when the day came."[24] The King watched some training exercises and demonstrations, and inspected the men to a musical accompaniment provided by the band of the Metropolitan Police. The Home Guard who, "back with the shoulders and keeping step with the best, stiff as ramrods on parade, marched past the saluting base [in front of the cricket pavilion] with the precision of Guards."[25] The March Past included representatives from the ARP Services, AFS, British Red Cross Society, Wolf Cubs and Scouts, and lasted 30 minutes. Others had a very private view of the proceedings through holes drilled in the doors of the cricket pavilion.

One of the demonstrations involved attacking, with Molotov Cocktails, a car driven down the slope where the bungalows in Bencurtis Park now stand. The driver jumped out at the bottom of the slope, leaving the Fire Brigade, who had prudently stationed a trailer pump nearby, to deal with the blazing wreck.

Two of the deacons from Emmanuel Church, members of the Home Guard, were detailed to fill sandbags on Corkscrew Hill, to appear to be working hard as the King passed by on his way to Glebe House. They filled a pile of sandbags, but the King was late in arriving so they sat down on the sandbags to take a short rest – of course the King passed by at that moment!

Page from a German invasion handbook

All through that summer there were constant air battles overhead. The proximity of Biggin Hill, Kenley and Croydon airfields ensured a grandstand view of events. Bob Squires had an even closer view. He was at that time a civilian driver employed by the Air Ministry and based at a depot at the rear of the Metropolitan Water Board's Pumping Station at Kent Gate where there were about 100 men whose job it was to repair the tarmac of the airfields in the area. On 18 August 100 German planes raided Biggin Hill aerodrome and dropped 200 bombs. One of the enemy planes was shot down in the vicinity but the pilot baled out and was captured at Layhams Farm.

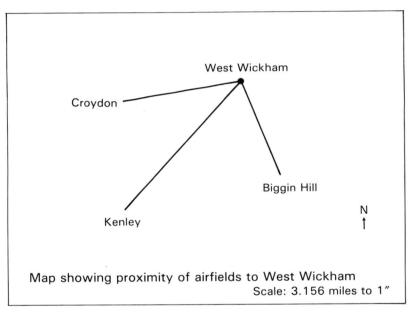

Map showing proximity of airfields to West Wickham
Scale: 3.156 miles to 1″

The constant air raids affected school attendances. On the morning of 23 August, because of an overnight alert, only 61 pupils presented themselves at Hawes Down School. Even fewer pupils attended on 2 September and they were sent home. The children were to spend long periods in the school shelters. Miss Audrey Thompson (now Hearne) was a teacher at Hawes Down Junior School during this period and recollects that part of the ground floor "was used as an ARP Centre and their Operations Room was below my classroom. With their acute hearing the children soon became aware of the signal of an impending air raid, and opened their desks, gathered their 'shelter' activities and stood up ready to march down before the siren sounded. There were limitations as to what one could do, we chanted tables, learned spellings, played word games, did mental arithmetic, the children read books and we read to them. They adapted very readily to the uncomfortable conditions.'' [26]

The School Log Book became a catalogue of air raid warnings.

3 September – No school because of air raid warnings.
5 September – Children in shelters 10–11.15, 3.05–4.35.
6 September – In shelters 9–10.
10 September – Air raid warning – 3.55. 20 minutes in trenches.
11 September – Two air raid warnings 11.50–12.10, 3.15–4.30.
13 September – 4 hours in shelter. 9.50–2 pm. Bottles of milk distributed to those who had ordered school milk. Biscuits were supplied to everyone. There was no afternoon school.
16 September – Short air raid warning in the morning. Four hours in the shelter in the afternoon, biscuits again supplied.
17 September – Two alerts during the day, each of one hour's duration.
18 September – Two short alerts in the morning, in the afternoon 1.15–2.30.
19 September – Two short visits to the shelter.
20 September – One short visit to the shelter. Attendance for the week averaged 47.7%.
23–30 September – Air raid warnings every day.

The children at Wickham Common School adapted to this new way of life just as easily as those at Hawes Down School. "We used to make a game of doing air raid drill in the classroom in case there was an attack before any warning siren had sounded. We urged the children to see who could be first in lying under their table supporting their chest off the floor with one elbow in case gun-fire should cause the floorboards to vibrate and possibly wound them.'' [27]

Enid Brooks (now Mrs. How) was a wartime pupil at Wickham Common School. She remembers that "at the sound of an air raid warning everyone filed into the shelters at the other end of the playground and each class had its own corridor to sit in. After 30 minutes in the shelter everyone had a packet of biscuits or a Horlicks tablet! Then there was the excitement when bombs fell in the playing field, and the craters became a source of wonder at the fossils that were exposed when the flints were blown apart.'' [28]

It was fun for the children, not so for their teachers with the awesome responsibility for children in wartime. Mercia Sansom recollects that at Wickham Common School "we spent many weary hours in the shelter. At first there were no lights in the shelter and every teacher was given a torch. But as the shelters were built in zig-zag patterns, when the teacher at the front of the line disappeared round a corner, the back of the class was in total darkness. Every child had to bring into the shelter, outdoor clothes – kept on the back of the chairs in the classroom – their gas mask and a small box containing two ear plugs, chewing gum (to put between the teeth during a raid to prevent biting the tongue) and a couple of Horlicks tablets for emergency rations. When lighting was installed we took books into the shelter, and with the children sitting on wooden benches against the wall and their feet in puddles, we endeavoured to continue their education."[29]

The adults in the neighbourhood obviously coveted these bankside shelters. "We began to find the local people in possession when we arrived at school in the morning and very often during that period when the endless rain provided cover for enemy bombers day and night, they were still emerging as we shepherded the children in."[30]

Teachers' responsibilities were not relinquished when the school day had finished. "Amazingly in these strange times life took on some sort of pattern. Teachers trained after school in First Aid and learned to distinguish between the smells of the different poison gases we were expecting to encounter. Field kitchens with brick chimneys were built in every playground which we were expected to operate if local bombing cut off food supplies."[31]

25 August   *First RAF raid on Berlin*

The transport system was frequently disrupted. Commuters on buses and trains found their routes somewhat circuitous at times. Connie Manser (now Winter) a civil servant "travelled in many different ways to get to London. I think I finished up in every terminus at various times. I even travelled in an open-backed lorry once, which had rows of chairs set out on it."[32] Ida Watson (later to write a history of West Wickham) described a journey from West Wickham that involved changing at Catford Bridge on to a bus to Lewisham. There were no trains running from Lewisham so the obliging bus driver took his charges to New Cross Gate. Eventually London Bridge was reached and a No. 10 bus completed the odyssey.

West Wickham was bombed for the first time on 31 August when 85 The Avenue, home of Mr. and Mrs. George Thompson, was badly damaged. Ida Watson recorded, "One house in Avenue down and next door rendered uninhabitable. Mrs. Thompson lived in latter."[33] The daughter of the house, Audrey Thompson, recalls that "the house next door was directly hit and most of it fell on ours. None of us was hurt, but we were shocked. The house was condemned and we returned only when it was rebuilt after the War. Then began a time of wandering around from place to place. We would get messages

40

'Do not go home, there is a land-mine in your garden' or 'There's an unexploded bomb near where you live.' I went so far as to carry my tooth-brush around with me.''[34]

On 6 September a Hurricane fighter from 303 Squadron was shot down and crashed in flames on Langley Park Golf Course.[35] The Polish pilot, Squadron Leader Zdzislaw Krasnodebski, baled out badly burned and was admitted to Farnborough Hospital. Station Officer Woodman was sent with a fire crew to deal with the incident. It was their first experience of dealing with a plane on fire, so with ammunition exploding all around, they approached the plane very cautiously through the mounds of earth and extinguished the fire.

On 7 September, a sunny summer's day, local people watched shortly after 4.15 pm as the skies overhead were filled with squadrons of German bombers on their way to London, the largest raid yet for months. For 57 nights the sound of enemy planes flying overhead became a familiar chilling noise. The docks and the East End were the targets on that first night, and incendiary bombs rained down. The blaze from the huge fires could be seen from Wickham. Ernest Garland of Silver Lane was officially commended by the King ''for gallantry during the heavy bombing of London docks . . . on the occasion of the enemy attack on the Surrey Commercial Docks . . . September 7 and 8, 1940.''[36] Ernest Garland had volunteered with

11. Surrey Commercial-Docks.

Surrey Docks. Photograph taken from a German invasion handbook others to form a First Aid Party with an ambulance, travelling to distant parts of the Docks which were almost inaccessible.

Firemen were mobilised from all around London and far beyond. At Old Jewry, Station Officer Woodman from Wickham went up to the Senior Officer and on asking which fire he and his crew were to tackle, was invited to take his pick! Two crews of local AFS men "with their pumps, were sent to West Ham around 7.30 pm and from there were ordered to the water-front at North Woolwich. Fires were everywhere, and as night wore on, row after row of dockers' houses were alight, but little could be done. The water mains were damaged and it was low tide on the Thames, so for several hours all that could be done was rescue pets and valuables for the people before the flames crept along the streets to their houses."[37]

7 September   *Code word CROMWELL is given – meaning 'invasion imminent'.*

In the early hours of 8 September an oil bomb and High Explosive bombs fell on Coney Hall where Warden Post 57 in Croydon Road was demolished. Seven wardens escaped without serious injury. The Post was next to the garden of the District Warden, Sydney Skipper who, when he got out, saw his lawn littered with incendiary bombs. Fortunately his own family was unharmed in an Anderson shelter at the end of the garden. Another bomb exploded a short distance away between two houses which were practically demolished. The wardens heard a woman shouting for help from underneath the wreckage, and despite their injuries, went to her assistance. Several houses and shops in the vicinity were also badly damaged. One car near the Post was completely wrecked and blown against the side of the house. There was thought to be an unexploded bomb close to the Coney Hill Children's Home, so the children were evacuated to the nearby Baptist Church.

On Friday 13 September bombs fell in the High Street; Ravenswood Avenue, partially demolishing No. 7; alongside 16 Braemar Gardens; Nos. 5–11 Ravenswood Crescent; Beckenham Road; and Station Road. Oscar Evans and his father Thomas were killed at 30 Station Road; Wilfred Horton and his family at 5 The Grove had to be rescued from their shelter. Another bomb landed on the courts of West Wickham Hard Courts Tennis Club – the blast broke windows at 116 Woodland Way, Emmanuel's Manse.

A bomb wrecked 47 Pine Avenue on the evening of 15 September and damaged No. 45 where the force of the explosion sent window frames hurtling over the tops of the houses on the other side of Pine Avenue into their back gardens. Another bomb fell at the rear of 55

Braemar Gardens badly damaging the house and burying prize apple trees.

17 September   *Hitler postpones the invasion of England.*

On 20 September a Molotov Breadbasket (a canister of incendiary bombs) bestrode Manor Road, Chessington Way and Bolderwood Way. An. H.E. bomb destroyed two houses in South Walk during a raid on Croydon aerodrome. The Rescue Services spent two hours digging for the occupants who later returned from a visit to the cinema! A land-mine fell in The Avenue, fortunately it failed to explode.

27 September   *Axis Pact signed. Germany, Italy and Japan are the signatories.*

On 27 September, 70 and 72 Queensway were destroyed by a Spitfire from 72 Squadron, shot down by an ME 109 over Sevenoaks. Flying Officer Paul Davies-Cooke baled out but he fell dead near Hayes Station.

Barry Leach, then a pupil at Greenhayes School, recalls the shooting down of the Spitfire in Queensway. He was "standing in the playground during mid-morning break and watching a dog-fight overhead from which a Spitfire crashed in Coney Hall, leaving its pilot drifting on a parachute. There had been no air raid warning but hearing the boys cheer when the pilot's parachute opened, Mr. Banister, the Headmaster, rushed out of the quiet seclusion of his study to call us into the improvised air raid shelter in the cloakroom."[38]

Many pilots from Biggin Hill made use of the hospitality afforded at The Warren in Croydon Road – among them, Alan Deere, R. Stanford-Tuck, Jamie Rankin, 'Sailor' A. G. Malan, C. Masterman, Don Kingaby, 'Spy' de la Torre and E. H. Thomas. Squadrons 32, 72, 92 and 610 were well represented and French, Belgian and Norwegian pilots' vocal talents were much in evidence when they sang songs around the piano. Pilots, putting in a late appearance after being thought missing from a sortie, were hoisted to the ceiling.

Women had adapted quickly to the upheaval of war – rationing, coping without their menfolk, voluntary work and air raids soon became part of the daily routine. Those living near West Wickham Fire Station found a very helpful aid close to hand with the knowledge that the firemen had very early warning of impending air raids. Station Officer Woodman remembers that "We had various alerts – yellow, red and purple for operating the siren. We had a lighting system to indicate to the manpower. On certain alerts you

Facsimile of signatures of RAF pilots and others   *The Warren*

had to get ready, some to prepare and others you had to put top boots on and immediately go out. The housewives in the locality got to know this and when they did their shopping, called in, asked if any warnings were on and if so, what colour? 'Just time to shop if a yellow . . .' The word went around – 'There's a yellow on!' One of the firemen was caught out by the system when he went down to Hoyler's in Red Lodge Road for a hair-cut. The siren went and he jumped out of the chair with only half his hair cut, to come running back on duty. What annoyed him was that after the All Clear he had to queue up to have the other half cut!"[39]

The Royal Observer Corps had set up a Post, Y1, on the roof of West Wickham Post Office before the War began. This Post was part of a network of 36 Posts controlled from the headquarters of No. 19 Group in Church Gardens, Bromley[40] which covered the whole of South-East England into London – the connecting link between the Posts and Fighter Command. Councillor John Collett, a chemist, was the Head Observer at Wickham and among his staff of volunteers, drawn largely from local businesses, were the manager of the Westminster Bank, Leslie Roe; Albert Everitt; Mr. Cushing; William Pett; G. W. Turner the greengrocer; and 'Steady Brown', sometime Wimbledon umpire. Members of this Post maintained observation on aeroplane activities right round the clock until mid 1945.

While West Wickham was denied the pleasure of having American G.I.s in the neighbourhood, their Canadian counterparts arrived in Wickham in September and were billeted mostly in Coney Hall. Mrs. Ivy Crier at 11 Layhams Road "had a nice bunch of lads next door and how they appreciated what little in the way of home cooking we could give them. The Canadians did have their own cookhouse at the other end of Layhams Road – No. 127. We had very happy times with the Canadians and . . . can't speak highly enough of them."[41]

The Canadian officers of the 3rd Field Regiment 92nd Battery made their headquarters in offices over the Temple Motors Garage. They and other ranks were officially welcomed by the Revd. C. A. Shaw Page during an entertainment in the Coney Hall. With the advent of the Canadians and their own Band, dances in the Coney Hall became much livelier and jitterbugging became all the rage. Professional artistes graced the boards – ENSA sent companies to entertain the troops and Geraldo and his Band filled the hall with their brand of music. Church Parades were held there with James Manser from Emmanuel Church on the piano and daughter Connie as a soloist. "It was the first time I heard 'O Canada' sung by a hall full of Canadian soldiers and I found it most moving."[42] Friendly relations were soon established, particularly with the young female members of the population. Gunner George Edward lost his heart to Florence Drewery of Layhams Road and they were married in St. John's Church on 21 December 1940. Baby Gordon arrived in 1941 and

Michael in 1943. Both babies were baptised in St. John's, the first of many Canadian offspring born and baptised in West Wickham during the war years.

Gunner Francis Boyd of the Canadian Army and Miss Joyce Fuller

John Merigan remembers the Canadian soldiers. Post wardens had to have precise numbers of occupants in every house in their areas in the event of a direct hit by a bomb. The Canadians would report their presence in a particular house for the night to the nearest Post. Such clandestine visits were discreetly noted by the wardens.

Station Officer Woodman remembers the Canadians too, for the fire hazards presented by those of them billeted in houses at the Addington Road end of Hawes Lane where fencing was ripped up for fuel. Picture rails of houses in and around Croft Avenue suffered a

46

similar fate. It must be said though that householders were generously compensated for the damage caused. The Canadians were generally well liked in West Wickham and their generosity to individuals in the way of luxuries was by way of thanks for the hospitality shown them. The fact that they were here to defend this area of Kent from aerial attack was of considerable comfort too.

Graves of civilian casualties buried in St. John's churchyard bear mute testimony to the indiscriminate nature of air attack. Not all deaths were caused by incidents occurring in West Wickham. Albert Boyden aged 45, of Silver Lane, was killed at Wandsworth on 9 September; Charles Hammond aged 47, was killed at Hayes; 40 year-old Frank Westropp lost his life at Sidcup; three members of the Elkins family of Copse Avenue, including five-year-old Elizabeth, were killed at Penge. The grandparents were killed in the same incident and are buried beside their daughter. St. Mary's Church Hall was used as a Rest Centre for those bombed out in and around the district. Every Saturday night a small band of the faithful turned the secular hall into a church.

In the early hours of 2 October bombs fell in Station Road, Wickham Crescent, MacAndrew Playing Field, Corkscrew Hill (where three people were killed), Stambourne Way, Wickham Court Road and Links Road. Mr. and Mrs. Percival Dray and their daughter Elsie were killed when 8 Links Road was completely demolished by an H.E. bomb. The Drays had no air raid shelter and slept on the ground floor. Their neighbours at No. 6, also destroyed, had gone to a public shelter. Despite the force of the explosion, windows only a few yards away remained intact.

Demolition squads at work in Wickham Crescent and Links Road were machine-gunned later that day but there were no reported casualties. On another occasion while George Raymond was instructing in the hut on Coney Hall Recreation Ground, a German plane flew in low from the direction of Wickham Court Farm where it had machine-gunned cattle and proceeded then to fire at those on the ground. The cattle were the only casualties.

John Merigan was by now Incident Officer at Post 50 which covered the area at the west end of the High Street. This Post was at first in temporary accommodation in the offices of Samson Salter, estate agents, on the corner of Manor Road at its junction with the High Street. Later a permanent Post was built at the rear of what is now the New Church opposite the Wheatsheaf. John Merigan recalls that "our first bomb hit the High Street and caused widespread damage to shop fronts but no loss of life. We escaped real damage until October when four shops and Woolworth's were more or less demolished by

32 Stambourne Way 1940 *Bromley Central Library*

32 Stambourne Way 1990 *Joyce Walker*

48

a 500lb bomb at 8 pm one evening I was fortunate to be in the next to one flat from this incident and had to crawl over debris to report the incident. My progress was so hampered by the loose state of the wreckage that the services arrived before I could report it, although I was only fifteen yards from the impact at the time of the hit."[43]

Post 50. Back row L – R: R. E. Mettrop, G. Askew, (?), Mrs. V. Taylor, J. Hunter, J. D'Eath, (?), M. Lake. Front row L – R: Mrs. M. Caine, Mrs. V. Killick, W. J. Merigan, Mrs. M. D'Eath, Mrs. Apps *John Merigan*

Children soon learned to seek out bomb incidents in order to collect firewood. Jean Colley (now Chamberlain) remembers the incident in the High Street because the Wool Shop was badly damaged. Canadian soldiers helping in clearing-up operations filled her basket with wood, but when she arrived home she found nestling among the firewood a pair of woollen gauntlets and some balls of wool!

Dorothy Wingent safe and snug with her family in the shelter in Manor Park Road remembers "how the walls of the shelter seemed to come into us."[44] Another of her memories, and a common one, was the acrid smell following a bomb explosion, the smell of plaster and the dust. Always there was dust.

On 7 October a bomb fell in the road between 58 and 60 Ravenswood Avenue, adjacent to St. Francis Church. It destroyed the East Window, the organ and the North Wall. The bomb crater was enormous, almost the width of the road itself and the force of the explosion hurled heavy masses of concrete incredible distances. One large piece of concrete crashed through the roof of the Odeon cinema next to the Post Office in Station Road, slightly injuring two soldiers. It seems that the patrons were not unduly alarmed but the performance had to be discontinued because light was showing through the hole in the roof. Another massive piece of concrete fell on the iron entrance-gate of St. Francis Church.

Bomb-damaged interior of St. Francis Church   *Revd. Owen Everson*

Shops in the High Street were hit again on that same day, severely damaging Nos. 81–83, the premises of Logan's the caterers and Treadwell's Shoe Shop. On 9 October a bomb fell outside Chettle's the opticians at No. 65, leaving a crater in the road. John Merigan was discussing the situation with Eric Chettle when, without thinking, someone discarded his cigarette in the crater. Up went the gas mains and those in the neighbourhood had to make do without gas for several days. Other bombs falling on 9 October badly damaged 21 and 23 Sherwood Way and houses in Station Road.

On the night of 11 October houses in South Walk, Addington Road and Queensway were hit and several houses demolished. At least fifteen bombs fell the following night, the craters extending for a mile or so, almost in a straight line. Three of them fell in the grounds of

50

Hawes Down School – one on tarmacadam close to some vehicles and an ambulance was burnt out; another hit a shelter and one of the occupants, a Mr. Joyce, was taken to hospital; the third bomb fell close to the canteen. A fourth bomb fell in a field and knocked down some wooden fencing. Backs of a number of houses in Pickhurst Rise were damaged by a fifth bomb. Another fell on the back of a house in Wickham Chase. Five more bombs fell on Langley Park Golf Course, the last ending at the 11th hole. Another fell in the front garden of a house in Barnfield Wood Road; two more fell in Wickham Way.

On 15 October, 25 Windermere Road was the scene of death and destruction. Mr. and Mrs. James Bevis and a Mrs. Wood were killed when the house was destroyed by an H.E. Bomb. Mrs. Mary Bevis survived initially but later succumbed to her injuries. Houses on either side were badly damaged. An oil bomb fell in the front garden of a house in Hawes Lane and another in The Avenue, during the same raid.

The fields at the rear of Wickham Court received bombs two nights running and St. John's West Window was badly damaged. Incendiaries also fell on Boleyn Gardens. Nos. 16–18 Bolderwood Way were hit on the night of 20–21 October. It was Coney Hall's turn on 23–24 October.

On Sunday morning 27 October, an ME 109 was shot down by RAF fighters, its fuselage and a wing falling in the middle of a field of mangolds on Wickham Court Farm.[45] The other wing with a gun still intact, crashed in the garden of 130 Woodland Way. It took seven ARP wardens to carry the wing and gun to the nearby West Wickham Hard Courts Tennis Club from whence it was removed by the RAF. Part of the tail and other fragments fell in the vicinity. The German pilot, Leutnant Wilhelm Busch, baled out and was captured, slightly wounded, at Addington. Noel Searle, an off duty policeman, walking across Sparrows Den at the time, ran for cover as the Messerschmitt plunged to earth. The shocked policeman picked some leaves from the tree that had given him shelter and placed them in his Bible.

Several bombs had fallen that day in back gardens of houses in Boleyn Gardens and Bramley Way. One of the last to fall partially demolished 27 Bramley Way, injuring Mr. and Mrs. Charles Barber and killing a relative.

On 29 October the cook and a maid were killed when the domestic quarters of the Coney Hill Children's Home were hit. Fortunately the 22 children were elsewhere in a sand-bagged room. They were quickly evacuated to the Rectory in Gates Green Road. The First Aid

252 & 254 Wickham Chase November 1940 *Bromley Central Library*

252 & 254 Wickham Chase 1990 *Joyce Walker*

52

Post in Wickham Common School was activated and Mercia Sansom had to divert her pupils' attention as stretcher cases were carried past the classroom window. The children from the Home were evacuated a few days later to Moss Home, Kimpton in Hertfordshire.

West Wickham Station was badly damaged by H.E.s on 1 November and the signal box was put out of action. Also on the receiving end were Red Lodge Road (where the Railway Hotel was badly damaged), Addington Road, Courtfield Rise, Coney Hall Recreation Ground, Wickham Chase and Hawes Lane. The following night, showers of incendiaries fell in the High Street, Bolderwood Way, Hawkhurst Way, Copse Avenue, Sherwood Way, Wickham Chase, Langley Way and Pickhurst Rise.

Tragedy was ever-present. The family of Sergeant/Pilot James White gathered at 45 Oaklands Avenue on the eve of his 21st birthday, unaware that the young ferry pilot had been killed the previous day. The sad news arrived after the celebrations had ended. Another pilot killed in a flying accident was Ronald Shayes, a British Davis Cup player and formerly a stretcher bearer at the Hawes Down ARP Depot.

Early on 20 November bombs fell in Wood Lodge Lane, Sparrows Den, Stambourne Way and Layhams Road where a concrete shelter was demolished. Ivy Crier was one of a team of fire-watchers in Layhams Road. Wearing a tin hat and armed with a stirrup pump, she "went up and down Layhams Road where pails of water and buckets of sand were left at the front gates . . ."[46]

Barry Leach who had watched the Spitfire crash on Coney Hall was an avid observer and collector of types of enemy aircraft. In November after bombs had straddled Stambourne Way, his mother took Barry and his brother Peter to stay with an aunt in the New Forest for a few weeks. Barry remembers their departure very clearly because on the way to the station there was an air raid in which the Italian Air Force made a contribution to the Battle against Britain. The young schoolboy excitedly added the Fiat BR 20 bomber and the Fiat CR 42 biplane to his observer's list. Since the Italian formation was being attacked by a squadron of Hurricanes and shed its load of bombs at that moment, Mrs. Leach did not share her son's enthusiasm at the experience.

On the night of 22 – 23 November it was the turn of Oaklands Avenue, Woodland Way, the grounds of the Heart Hospital and Nash Farm to be bombed. The 8 December saw incendiaries falling on Coney Hall and three H.E.s on the northern part of Wickham – one on the children's playground in Blake Recreation Ground and the other two in Ravenswood Avenue and Ravenswood Crescent.

Amid this maelstrom of events the Women's Institute kept going, urged on at one meeting by a speaker who said that to find things normal at an Institute would be a really steadying influence. At that same meeting a list was given of the variety of interests pursued by the West Wickham WI in wartime: funds raised for the Federation Ambulance; drama; whist drives for war funds; a National Savings Group; fruit bottling; a large number of woollen garments sent to the Deep Sea Fishermen; Red Cross work; First Aid; ARP and canteen work; the preparation of ration books; manning the salvage showroom in the High Street; and the delivering of circulars.

Something else constant and indeed, flourishing, was the pastime of dancing. It was a form of relaxation, an antidote to the stress of everyday survival. There were regular dances in the Lecture Hall, the Coney Hall, over the Temple Motors Garage and even in the Fire Station. Others found an outlet in sporting activities. Leslie Roe found solace in his piano. It led indirectly to saving a policeman from injury during a raid. One evening while the bank manager was playing his favourite Moonlight Sonata, a bomb fell near the bank. Next morning a uniformed policeman asked to see him – "You did me a good turn last night. I stood on your front doorstep listening to your piano during our raid . . ."[47] and was thus protected from the blast of the bomb.

During the winter, Hungary, Rumania and Bulgaria join Germany and Italy. In late October Italy attacks Greece from occupied Albania. In Africa the Italian Army attacks the British Commonwealth Forces.

There were by now, shortages of almost every commodity. Tom Wingent, a glass-blower, worked in rented accommodation over an empty shop at 12 High Street, where he produced coloured glass balls for Christmas tree decorations. They sold like wildfire.

It was a time of mixed fortunes for local firemen. Having served valiantly in Wickham and London, they responded to a call from Manchester for assistance when that city was bombed on 22 and 23 December. Locked and deserted commercial buildings were on fire (fire-watching was not yet compulsory), Manchester Cathedral was damaged, 75,000 houses damaged and 1,000 people killed. It was into this situation that at 20 minutes notice, Station Officer Woodman led 32 men. The pumps were already in Manchester so the local crews travelled to the city by bus, where they worked for 36 hours until relieved. Given the option of resting, they declined and journeyed home on Christmas Day, again by bus, blackened by smoke, dishevelled and exhausted. Unbelievably, transport cafes on the route declined to serve the firemen so it was not until they reached South

Mimms that they were able to quench their thirst! Fortunately they had been issued with iron rations – tinned corned beef, chocolate and hard biscuits. Eventually Wickham was reached and after the necessary ablutions there was blessed sleep. Certainly a Christmas to remember.

On the night of 29 December thousands of incendiaries were dropped on the City of London in the space of three hours. It was to be labelled the Second Fire of London – the red glow in the skies was visible from West Wickham. Once more, fire-crews were despatched from West Wickham to help in fighting the fires. One crew was sent to Tooley Street on the other side of the river where after three hours work it was possible to heat soup on the engine of the pump, it was so hot!

The next morning the garden of the Westminster Bank in the High Street was littered with charred fragments of bibles and prayer books, blown by the wind from a City church.

And so 1940 came to a fiery close. 1941 promised more of the same.

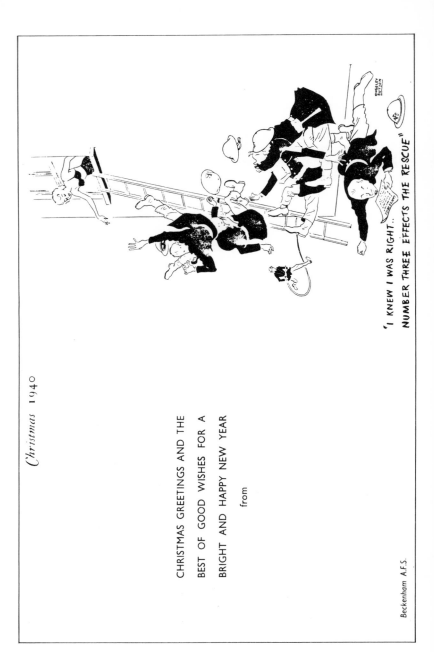

Christmas 1940

CHRISTMAS GREETINGS AND THE

BEST OF GOOD WISHES FOR A

BRIGHT AND HAPPY NEW YEAR

from

Beckenham A.F.S.

"I KNEW I WAS RIGHT... NUMBER THREE EFFECTS THE RESCUE"

4. *1941*

"The five comrades were laid to rest in one grave in West Wickham Churchyard . . ."

Kentish Times March 1941

Regulations for a compulsory Fire Watch system for business premises were introduced under which men between the ages of 16 and 60 had to register for fire-watching 48 hours a month. In Wickham there had already been unofficial fire-watch teams, one of them organised by Mrs. Lilian Pain from the premises of Richer's in the High Street. Fire-watch teams were organised at Emmanuel Church – its members on duty one night in every three weeks. One of the teams consisted of two seventeen-year-olds, Marjorie Moyce and Connie Manser, and a deacon, Mr. Bill Ware. Up to this time Emmanuel Church had escaped relatively lightly from enemy action. There was one fire caused by a firework thrown through a window in 1941 that had serious consequences for the Ladies Sewing and Social Party. The firework lodged under the cupboard where the ladies kept all their precious materials which had to be bought with clothing coupons, and everything was burnt. There were sewing machines and cottons, embroidery silks and paper patterns which were almost impossible to replace. The group took a long time to recover from the fire.

The response at St. John's Church to a request from the rector for volunteers was negligible. It could have been disastrous for the church, for on 11 January incendiaries fell, one of which struck the main roof and glanced off into the lead gutter surrounding the organ chamber. The timbers were alight when Patrol Officer Evan Butler discovered the fire. He climbed up the wall and working single-handed, extinguished the fire and so saved a priceless heritage for West Wickham. A grateful rector afterwards made a presentation to the brave and resourceful fireman. More incendiaries rained down on Wickham on 5 February, and on the last day of the month a bomb fell on Sylvan Way.

Meanwhile work continued on the construction of a connecting link road between Ravenswood Crescent and Manor Park Road. Road construction had been halted by the War but there was a need for a second route to Croydon should the High Street be blocked by enemy action.

Members of the British Red Cross Society were kept busy at all times. Some of the VADs worked two or three days a week at Lewisham Hospital where one of them, Mrs. Florence Steele, told how when the sirens sounded, most of the patients were moved to places of safety, but that those unable to be moved had enamel washing bowls placed on their heads for protection. Mrs. 'Buddy' Abbott served at Farnborough Hospital and also assisted the District Nurse; she also taught First Aid to the Army Units stationed at Wickham Court. Other Red Cross VADs classified as 'mobile', as distinct from 'immobile', were posted to Chatham Naval Hospital, Cambridge Military Hospital, Ilford Mobile Ambulance Unit, RAMC Emergency Base Hospitals and the Royal Naval Hospital at Plymouth. Others were seconded to First Aid Posts at Elmers End and the Hawes Down Clinic. Assistance was also given at local hospitals.

Many of the Red Cross personnel were, as others, seeing war service for the second time in their lives. Florence Steele had been a ledger clerk with the WRAF; Mrs. Edith Salchow had previously served with a London VAD Detachment; Sister Florence Cherrill, the Nursing Officer of Kent 82 Detachment, had been a nurse with the Scottish Women's Nursing Service at the Scottish Women's Hospital in Royaumont, France.

Civil Defence Services subject to compulsory enrolment. Registration of Employment Act. Individuals now directed towards essential war work. Applicable to women of 20 and 21.

Bombs fell on the edge of Well Wood (part of which was requisitioned by the military authorities) on 9 March, and on the following day on Spring Park Woods and Ravenswood Avenue. Ten days later Cherry Tree Walk (where Nos. 1 and 3 were destroyed), Lime Tree Walk, Queensway, Pickhurst Rise and Goodhart Way were bombed. The bomb that landed on Queensway exploded in the middle of the road below the surface, making an enormous crater but despite that, no windows were broken on either side of the road. One gentleman in a nearby shelter had his false teeth blown out by the blast! They were eventually found buried in the earth floor of the shelter.

Distribution begins of the new indoor Morrison table shelter. It is free to those earning no more than £350 per annum plus allowances for children. It goes on sale for £8.

1 & 3 Cherry Tree Walk 1990 *Joyce Walker*

Merchant ships are being sunk at the rate of three a day. Food shortages are at their worst. Dried eggs and dried milk are imported from the USA. Chickens are kept in back gardens – fed on meal, scraps and potato peelings. Others keep rabbits. Pig Clubs are set up.

Mrs. Irene Roe lived in the flat over the Westminster Bank and has vivid memories of the egg situation: "Dried eggs were useful but not like real eggs, so ever experimental, I bought four hens from Cook's Farm at Keston – and so gave us a great deal of excitement, worry, but a lot of eggs when they were in lay. Our dear Mr. Govier, Wickham's expert gardener helped prepare nesting boxes and a small wired run. One sunny day they were delivered, let loose and promptly took flight over the high brick wall, up The Grove and into a lime tree. Only four, it seemed like twenty-four! They were caught, helped by very amused passers-by, settled at last . . ."⁴⁸

A Pig Club based at Smith's Dairy Farm and organised by Councillor Mrs. Catherine Bellringer, raised large sums of money for the Red Cross Prisoner-of-War Fund. Another Pig Club was run by the personnel of the Hawes Down ARP Depot, on allotments in Hawes Lane. Later in the year it became obvious that it was of the utmost importance to store all possible foodstuffs for cattle in the coming

"WE WILL REMEMBER THEM"

KILLED IN ACTION — 19-3-1941

WESLEY DREW

DENNIS FITZGERALD

FREDDIE MOORE

LES. PALMER

BOB SHORT

winter. To that end haymakers were to be seen at work in Sparrows Den where eventually a haystack appeared, a reminder of the country village of the past. Yet another reminder was the sight of cattle grazing on the football pitch adjacent to the footpath through the West Wickham Playing Fields.

Wardens were kept busy, not only dealing with the effects of air raids, but also ensuring that houses and business premises were kept darkened after dusk. Fines were imposed in the courts for allowing lights to be visible. Mrs. 'Dolly' Stiff was fined 30 shillings for allowing a light to be seen in her flat over Lloyds Bank at 8.40 pm on 19 March. Dolly Stiff was most apologetic, having been on duty at an Aid Post at the time. People wore items which would make them visible in the black-out. Marjorie Moyce (later to join the Women's Land Army) wore a 'luminous gardenia' in her lapel – apparently it was not very effective.

The London Fire Brigade, under intense pressure still, had frequently to call for reinforcements from outlying areas. It was on one such occasion on 19 March at West Ham that five Coney Hall AFS men lost their lives. They comprised the crew of a pump, one of a convoy on the way to a fire at Silvertown, which was obliterated in a land-mine explosion in Plaistow Road. Wesley Drew, Stanley Short, Frederick Moore, Dennis Fitzgerald and Leslie Palmer were buried in one grave in St. John's churchyard. A saddened Coney Hall mourned the loss of its young men but there was more to come. Just four weeks later on 19 April while firemen were mustering for orders in a four-storey building, Old Palace School at Poplar, the building received a direct hit. Part of the building was demolished and a fire ensued, killing 34 firemen, 21 of them from the Beckenham Brigade. Ten of those 21 were attached to West Wickham Fire Station, six of them from West Wickham itself. Robert Deans, Kenneth Bowles, Cecil Farley, Martin Parfett and Percy Aitchison were buried in a mass grave at Beckenham Cemetery. Norman Mountjoy was buried with his brother-in-law, Ernest Beadle of Beckenham, in one grave next to their colleagues in St. John's churchyard.

There was to be no respite for the depleted crews in West Wickham and Beckenham. Plymouth was subjected to air attack five times in April and local crews were sent to assist.

There were firewomen at all Fire Stations by now. Gladys and Claire Williams (no relation) were at West Wickham. It had been decreed that firewomen were to be called by their surnames, so it was fortunate that Gladys and Claire were on different watches. Even so it was necessary to address them as 'Red' Willie and 'White' Willie. Leading Firewoman Eileen Rogers was transferred from Control Room duties at Beckenham to Wickham in 1941. She was known as 'Roge' and she remembers that "at West Wickham the women worked in the Station Watch Room where there was a switchboard and direct telephone lines to the sub Station who reported all incidents to us. There was also a Fire Alarm Board connected to the various fire alarms in the district. There was a Mobilising Officer in charge of the Watch Room. He dealt with the despatch of appliances to fires and incidents. I was his assistant . . . At that time we worked 48 hours on and 24 hours off . . . We had a flat over a shop opposite the Fire Station where we slept in bunks, about four or five of us to a room . . .''[49]

Connie Manser was called-up into the AFS with about a dozen other girls. "We did our training at the Fire Station in Glebe Way and this was taken very seriously, especially the physical training and the demonstrations of 'hook ladder drill' up the tower! We took an examination at the end of the training and were then given uniforms, and we did a night duty once a week in the control room. I was sent to Shortlands Station, which was a big house in Shortlands Road . . .''[50]

6 April	*Germany invades Yugoslavia and Greece where 60,000 British troops have landed.*
16 April	*Heaviest air raid so far on London, killing 1,200 civilians.*

At least twenty large bombs fell on West Wickham on Wednesday 16 April when the Civil Defence was tested to its limits. H.E.s fell on Cherry Tree Walk, Chestnut Avenue, 17 and 19 Birch Tree Avenue (destroyed), Queensway, Coney Hall Recreation Ground, Coney Hill Road (where six Canadian soldiers were killed), Gates Green Road, Robins Grove, Harvest Bank Road, Glebe Way, Wickham Court Road, The Mead, Pickhurst Rise, Langley Way, Pickhurst Lane, Goodhart Way, 7 and 9 Hayes Chase, Hartfield Crescent, a field at the rear of Smith's Farm, Manor Road, Grosvenor Road, Manor Park Close, Wickham Chase and Langley Park Golf Club. Several fires were caused by incendiaries as well as H.E.s and some developed into serious fires – at 4 The Avenue, Ravenswood Avenue, Wickham Court Farm, 203 High Street, 165 Queensway, 18 Rodney Gardens and 95 Harvest Bank Road. At Wickham Court Farm where farm buildings were set alight, a second H.E. cut the line of fire hoses from Layhams Road. The farm was hit yet again while the fires were still raging, but the Fire Brigade was overstretched and unable to re-lay more hoses. A large H.E. landed in a field off Layhams Road but failed to explode. An oil bomb and an incendiary fell on 41 Cherry

Grosvenor Road 1941 *Bromley Central Library*

Tree Walk, the ensuing fire completely destroying the house. Oil covered the garden including the pond where several goldfish succumbed.

John Merigan remembers that night. "Our Area Post 50 had 100s of incendiary bombs dropped. The High Street was ablaze with them and most of Manor Park Road and Manor Park Close had one in each house. People rallied round and followed our example of shovelling any bomb that entered the house . . . through the window and outside . . . just covered with earth. On that night Grosvenor Road was hit by two 500lb bombs. One of our Wardens [James Pyle] was taking his son to a shelter when a clump of clay weighing over a ton from a nearby bomb crater, crashed through his roof and completely destroyed the house [No. 13]"[51]

The roof of Langley Park Golf Club's clubhouse was badly damaged by incendiaries but "members put on a brave face . . . decided that the bar should remain open during air raids."[52] Elsewhere on the course sheep grazed contentedly (most of the time) on the lush pastures.

There must have been many brave deeds performed that night but only one seems to have come to the attention of the authorities. Corporal Fred Thew of 'A' Company 55 Kent Bn Home Guard, who together with two colleagues, rescued eight people from bombed buildings, was later rewarded with the Home Guard Certificate of Good Service.

The Civil Defence barely had time to gather breath from the 'Wednesday' when on the following Saturday there was another heavy raid involving loss of life at Wickham Chase. On the night of 22 April an unexploded bomb was found at 41 The Mead. Nearby schools were closed and the area evacuated until the bomb was made safe.

10 May   *Last and worst night of the London blitz – 1,436 killed.*

The railway station was damaged in a raid on 10 May. Other bombs in that same raid badly damaged 131 and 243 Langley Way and killed eight people in Pickhurst Rise: Mr. and Mrs. William Linnett and their eighteen-year-old daughter Joan at No. 108; Mr. and Mrs. George Gosling at No. 110; Mr. and Mrs. Frederick Nicholls at No. 112; and an un-named female at No. 126. Among those injured was fourteen-year-old Victor Gosling who was blown into a tree and paralysed from the waist down He died five years later in Stoke Mandeville Hospital, having been awarded the Cornwell Badge for bravery – a Scout award.

The bombs in Pickhurst Rise made several craters in the road, the most serious of which fractured a gas main at the junction with Langley Way. It was a brilliant moonlight night and the flames from the burning gas could be extinguished only by plugging with wet clay thrown up from the craters, which, incidentally, made access by road from Red Lodge Road impossible. The Rescue and Fire Services were forced to travel via The Avenue and down Pickhurst Rise from the other end.

Amid the tragedies there were lighter moments. Mrs. Eileen Preston of Langley Way rushed out of her home after the incidents in Pickhurst Rise and stood talking to a neighbour, truly a gentleman, before realising that she was clad only in her nightdress.

24 May   *HMS Hood sunk by the Bismarck*

Barry Leach, a Greenhayes pupil, remembers the sinking of *HMS Hood.* "In 1941 several of the older boys were allowed to visit the ARP Post established in a room on the west side of the school. I well recall Mrs. Chamberlain of Glebe House, who was manning the Post, calling us in to hear on mid-day radio, news that *HMS Hood,* the largest ship in the Royal Navy, had been sunk by the *Bismarck.*"[53]

27 May   *Bismarck sunk*
1 June   *Evacuation of British and Greek Forces from Crete completed.*

64

Greenhayes School pupils 1943 *Greenhayes School*

8 June   *Syria entered by British and French Forces.*
                  Clothes rationing begins.

The defensive role of the Home Guard changed from time to time. As has already been explained, the 55th Kent Bn was part of the outer defence zone of London including the anti-tank line, but later came the defence of Priority Open Spaces – Beckenham Place Park, Langley Park Golf Course, Biggin Hill aerodrome and the area around Layhams Farm. Exercises reflected the changes. There was the epic when No. 13 Platoon " . . . fought a rousing rearguard action, moving and transporting guns by manhandling from Layhams Farm to Wickham Court Farm."[54] Exercise 'Blue Nose' involved 'paratroops' who dropped around Wickham Court Farm right in the line of fire from No. 14 Platoon who had been instructed only to report. The paratroops who had been observed at Layhams Farm, proceeded in the direction of Fairchildes cross-roads where the Home Guard Machine-Gun Company and an infantry post were stationed (also 'on report only'). Canadian and other troops with Bren Guns and tanks, clattered by the unseen Home Guards. "From out of the blue came a YMCA van and proceeded to dispense tea to the garrison at Layhams Farm . . . it pushed off to the cross-roads where the garrison there, in the act of sampling tea and cakes were promptly captured . . ."[55]

22 June   *Germany invades Russia*

65

'Holidays at Home' were encouraged. One of the attractions on the cricketing scene was the visit by a British Empire team who played West Wickham in front of an 800 strong crowd. The visitors' team comprised A. A. Avery (Essex), T. H. Barling (Surrey), A. E. Nutter (Lancs), H. M. D. Forde (Barbados), J. F. Parker (Surrey), D. Donnelly (Assam), E. D. Eytle (British Guiana), L. R. Phillips (BBC), C. B. Clarke (West Indies), and K. B. Croker (Surrey). West Wickham Cricket Club at this time was not able to play regularly but as and when opportunities occurred.

Cheese rationed

12 July   *Britain and Russia enter into a Mutual Assistance Pact.*

Two RAF pilots were buried in St. John's churchyard on successive days in August – 21 year-old Sergeant/Pilot Gordon Parry of Cherry Tree Walk and Sergeant/Pilot Gordon Chugg of Gates Green Road. For the Parry family it was the second blow to fall within a few months. Gordon Parry senior, a Home Guard, had been badly injured when the headquarters of 'B' Company in Coney Hill Road was damaged in the raid on 16 April. "We had the terrible news that my brother Gordon, who was a pilot with Bomber Command, was killed. His plane had come down in Wales . . . It was like a terrible nightmare. Unfortunately though it was one that we would never awake from, for life was never to be quite the same for any of us again." [56]

18 August   *Problems caused by differences in the organisation and equipment of 1,400 separate fire brigades lead to the nationalisation of the Fire Service – NFS.*
25 August   *British and Russian Forces enter Persia.*

Civil Defence had become a compulsory service and there were many gaps to be filled. It was the same situation in the ranks of the Home Guard where members had been called up for active service. It was not yet compulsory for women to enlist in the Services but there were many volunteers. Margaret Balaam volunteered for the WAAF in 1941 and was able to join the Motor Transport section as a driver. She trained at Cardington on Ford 8s and six-wheeler lorries. She says that she passed her test despite crashing every gear! Margaret's first posting was to Blackpool in a very cold winter but sleeping on straw palliasses was not what she had in mind so she applied for and got a transfer to Market Drayton.

Joan Walker joined the WAAF as a volunteer a year later and qualified as a Group 2 FME (Flight Mechanic Engines). From working on Oxfords, Joan graduated to a Wellington bomber as the only woman in a team of eight. Much later she was re-graded because of knee problems brought about by the nature of her work. She passed a course in meteorology and thereafter served at Hendon and Croydon aerodromes.

Joan Walker was (and still is) a member of St. Francis' congregation. She and others were delighted when a replacement organ for the one destroyed in an air raid, was transferred from St. Mary's, Ramsgate in August. Dr. George Grace, the church organist, gave a short recital before the evening service on 29 August.

26–27 September   8th Army formed

Death came in all its forms – natural, accidental and violent. In September Mrs. Beatrice Shaw Page was killed in an accident in the Rectory. Her husband was dealt a double blow four months later when his bomber pilot son was reported missing after a raid on Brest. The body of Flying Officer Henry Shaw Page was later washed ashore on the Cornish coast.

A meeting of the Beckenham WVS was held in the Toc H hall for the purpose of opening a WVS Sub Office in West Wickham. Florence Quaif was nominated and subsequently confirmed as the local organiser. She and her ladies were soon involved in the communal feeding facilities set up in the Yew Tree Restaurant opened in Glebe Way. The Restaurant was adapted from three shops, seated 130 customers and staffed by WVS volunteers, who were supported by a paid staff of a cook and three kitchen maids. On the menu on the opening day in November were: soup; meat pie, greens and potatoes; rice pudding and stewed apple; tea; bread and butter – all for 11½d.! It proved to be a successful venture, providing cheap supplements to scanty rations.

National Savings Groups were now a way of life, not least in the schools. By November 1941 the Hawes Down Junior School's Group had collected £3,052 18s. 6d. Other young people were contributing to the war effort. At the Annual General Meeting of the Scout Association in Beckenham, reports of the year's activities included messenger service, waste paper salvage collection, the erection of Morrison table shelters and acting as stretcher-bearers.

Almost all salvageable material was collected for use in the war effort. Iron railings were sacrificed, either donated or requisitioned. Appeals against requisition were allowed and St. Francis Church succeeded in retaining its ornamental cast-iron railings on the grounds of historic and artistic merit, they having originated from old Church House at Westminster. The boundary railings at the Coney Hall Recreation Ground adjoining Layhams Road went in the cause.

68

Grave of Flight Lieutenant Henry Shaw Page DFC *Brian Etheridge*

Depots for the reception of waste metal, paper, even bones were arranged in nearly every road. The Women's Constitutional Association collected medicinal herbs and the Women's Institute arranged an outing to pick blackberries for the fruit preserving centre. Wolf Cubs collected rose-hips – turned by the manufacturers into syrup as a source of Vitamin C. Hawes Down School collected three cwts. of horse chestnuts.

(opposite, left)   Sergeant/Pilot Gordon Parry *Pauline James*

(opposite, right)   Margaret Balaam WAAF *Margaret Mayes*

Railings outside St. Francis Church   *Joyce Walker*

18 November	*British offensive in Libya begins.*
	Introduction of 'Points' coupons for certain types of tinned and dried foods.
2 December	*Full conscription of women.*
	Unmarried women between 20 and 30 subject to call-up. Choice between Services, Civil Defence and industry. Women up to 40 to register at an Employment Exchange for war work unless there are heavy family responsibilities.

A club was opened in the small Lecture Hall in Sussex Road with social and recreational facilities for soldiers and their friends. A year later another Services Club was opened in the Rectory in Gates Green Road. Canadian troops billeted in Wickham Court challenged local NFS men to darts matches.

6 December	*Russians launch counter-attack on Germany Army which retreats.*
7 December	*Japanese bombers attack United States Pacific Fleet in Pearl Harbour. USA declares war on Japan and other Axis Powers. Britain and her Allies declare war on Japan. Within six months, Japan captures the Philippines, Malaya, Singapore, Hong Kong, Burma, the Dutch East Indies and several British U.S. islands in the Pacific. India and Australia are now under threat of invasion.*

9 December   *Call-up age for men lowered to eighteen.*
11 December   *Germany and Italy declare war on USA.*

On Christmas Eve Gunner Sydney White of the Canadian Army married Mavis Biffin of Gates Green Road, in St. John's Church. This was the seventeenth wedding ceremony in the church during 1941 involving Canadian soldiers. The Canadian Anglican chaplain, Captain J. J. McKinney officiated at twelve of them.

There was a Christmas party for the boys of the Aberdare Memorial Home, at the Methodist Church Hall. The boys "as usual attended Divine Service in St. John's Eden Park."[57] At St. Francis Church a Carol Service was held in the afternoon of Christmas Day during which the congregation was able to listen to the King's speech.

25 December   *Hong Kong surrenders to the Japanese.*

Original AFS Memorial 1942

Unveiling of replacement memorial *Oliver Woodman*

5. 1942

"From Monday February 9th soap may be bought only against a coupon or buying permit."

Government directive

Boys and girls of sixteen to eighteen years of age are asked to help in the war effort by joining a youth organisation or a junior service unit. By 1942 almost every commodity is rationed including sweets.

20 January   Japan invades Burma

Parents had become accustomed to not sending their children to school because of air raids. Now there were other reasons. Heavy snow fell in January and February and this, combined with an epidemic of measles, made attendance figures much lower than usual. Warmth too was at a premium with a shortage of fuel. The continuing call-up of staff did not help the situation. Hawes Down Senior School lost R. W. Usher to the RAF and J. Rees to the East Surrey Regiment in January. The strain on the remaining teachers was immense, for not only were they trying to maintain educational standards, they were additionally involved in Civil Defence or fire-watching duties.

Only three months after his marriage to Joan Harvey at Emmanuel Church, Sergeant Sydney Peters, wireless operator/air gunner, was killed on 21 January 1942. He now rests in St. John's churchyard.

Single bananas and onions are used as raffle prizes.
Boys aged seventeen to register particulars about themselves to local offices.

15 February   Singapore surrenders to the Japanese.
16 February   Compulsory enrolment in the Home Guard. The lowest rank previously styled 'Volunteer' is now 'Private'.

In March six young boys from Coney Hall went for a walk to Skid Hill, Fairchildes, the site of an Army Training Ground. They picked up and took home fifteen unexpended smoke bombs and four two-inch trench mortar bombs. One of these exploded while four of the boys were examining them in the porch of 113 Layhams Road. Three of the boys were killed outright and the fourth was dead on arrival at hospital. Those killed were all from Layhams Road: Ken Dulley (117), Donald Fothergill (113), Alan Wilkins (73) and Montagu Baker (65).

Coney Hall suffered further tragedy in March when four-year-old Derek Knell and three-year-old John Wells were drowned in the pond adjoining vacant land by the Temple Motors Garage.

8 March   *Rangoon falls to the Japanese*
28 March   *St. Nazaire raid.*

As if the recent months had not been enough to bear, there was a reminder of the events of the previous year when a memorial was unveiled in St. John's churchyard to the five AFS men killed at West Ham.

The top floor of Springfield was converted to a Day Nursery. It was open from 7 am to 7 pm, at a cost of one shilling per child per day. Local firemen made toys for the children. Mrs. Christine Squires was especially glad to make use of the nursery for her two young sons. It was not easy running the family timber yard in wartime with a husband in the Army. Ever resourceful, Christine Squires bought and de-nailed packing cases which had contained aircraft; railway sleepers were cut up into 2 × 1 and she was able to supply firewood, sawn up by herself and sold in 1lb bundles. "She worked like five men."[58]

Coal is in short supply. Every family is urged to save fuel.
By mid 1942 all men aged 18–51 are liable to call-up to the Forces.

24 June   *Germans advance 50 miles across Egyptian border.*

It was an anxious time for those with relatives missing in the Far East. There was no news of David Waite of Woodland Way, a civilian who was editor of the Singapore Free Press. Better news came to the relatives of Gunner Leslie Jones of Sherwood Way, missing since the fall of Singapore – he was a prisoner-of-war in Japanese hands. In another theatre of the War, Sergeant Arthur Church of Church Drive, was still unaccounted for after the fall of Tobruk. Also missing were Sapper Norman Brooks of Chestnut Avenue and Bombardier Alan Gurney of Silver Lane.

1 July   *Germans reach El Alamein*
4 July   *American Air Force launches its first air attack against*
                 Germany.
                 British convoy PQ 17, taking supplies to Russia, is
                 largely destroyed.

74

Summer meant cricket. The Bromley Police Cricket Club was particularly strong and as such, entertained RAF representative sides at The Warren in Croydon Road. In August 1942 the RAF assembled O. Greenwood (Yorks), R. Mordount (I. Zingari, MCC), F. C. Dickinson (West Scotland), R. J. Gregory (Surrey), C. Oakes (Sussex), Ted Drake (Hants), L. J. Todd (Kent), A. C. Grass (Leics), E. Lambert (Yorks), R. Wilson (Sussex), T. Wilson (Yorks), Sergeant Faulkner (New South Wales) and A. C. Beardsley (Leics).

RAF v Bromley Police 1942   *Joe Sirett*

Audrey Thompson organised and became Commandant of a Girls Training Corps. She was assisted by two fellow teachers, Mercia Sansom and Joyce Draycott. Boys who were interested in aircraft, joined the Air Training Corps, 386 Squadron based at Beckenham. There were enough cadets from Wickham to warrant two training evenings a week at Hawes Down School.

Some missing servicemen were reported as being prisoners-of-war. Gunner Ernest Willis, Bombardier Alan Gurney, Trooper Donald Stuart and Sergeant Frederick Holder were held in Italy. Guardsman William Walker was also reported captured. Still missing since the fall of Singapore were Bombardier Frank Keenor and Sergeant Arthur Bellringer. Baby Anthony Bellringer was baptised in St. John's Church in June, his grandmother Catherine standing proxy for her other soldier son, Edward.

Girls Training Corps *Audrey Hearne*

From September 1942 until 1945 Wickham Court was home to HQ Company of the 27th A.A. Brigade. Fortunately for West Wickham the Brigadier relished the idea of living in such surroundings, so he involved his staff in the care and protection of the building. Not all country houses survived occupation and such hard usage. The stables became the motor transport yard and the greenhouses were cannibalised to make one good greenhouse, thus enabling tomatoes and other salad vegetables to be added to the canteen menu. The garden and woodland were brought back into good order and the great yew hedge and the two yew peacocks were re-cut. The garden area was totally replanted from packets of seeds and the kitchen garden put into a productive state. The tennis court was restored thanks to the specialised knowledge of one of the despatch riders of the attached signals unit. The tarmac area in front of the gates witnessed several ceremonial parades. On a less exalted plane it also hosted many games of basketball which were the daily morning exercise of the whole HQ staff from the Brigadier and the Senior Commandant ATS to the cookhouse orderly.

8th Army, led by General Montgomery, defeats the German and Italian armies at El Alamein and drives them out of Egypt. The church bells are allowed to ring to hail the first great turning point of the War.

76

Wickham Court Hotel

For some children, wartime conditions were the only way of life that they had ever known and human nature asserted itself. "Police Inspector Broad spoke to the children . . . with regard to damage to trees, allotments etc."[59] Another schoolmaster departed to serve his country – L. J. Turner joined the Royal Navy.

8 November   *American and British Forces land in French North Africa.*

The year had begun with the fall of Singapore but with the British victory at El Alamein, the landings in North Africa, 1,000 bomber raids on Germany and the threat of invasion receding, the tide seemed to be turning at last. The price exacted from West Wickham grew steadily. At least sixteen servicemen and 42 civilians (including Civil Defence personnel) had been killed and 25 prisoners in enemy hands. This relatively new community was being bonded in a way that it never could have envisaged.

Certificate of Proficiency
HOME GUARD

On arrival at the Training Establishment, Primary Training Centre or Recruit Training Centre, the holder must produce this Certificate at once for the officer commanding, together with Certificate A if gained in the Junior Training Corps or Army Cadet Force.

PART I. I hereby certify that (Rank) L/Cpl. (Name and initials) SHERIDAN.P.H.

of 'A' ~~Battery~~ 55th. Kent ~~Regiment~~ HOME GUARD has qualified
        Company   Battalion
in the Proficiency Badge tests as laid down in the pamphlet "Qualifications for, and Conditions governing the Award of the Home Guard Proficiency Badges and Certificates" for the following subjects :—

	Subject	Date	Initials
1.	General knowledge (all candidates)	22/10/43	
2.	Rifle	22/10/43	
3.	36 M Grenade	22/10/43	
4.	(a) Other weapon Northover Projector	22/10/43	
	(b) ~~Signalling~~		
5.	(a) Battlecraft, ~~(b) Coast Artillery, (c) Heavy A.A. Bty. work, (d) "Z" A.A. Battery work, (e) Bomb Disposal, (f) Watermanship, (g) M.T.~~	22/10/43	
6.	(a) Map Reading, ~~(b) Field works, (c) First Aid~~	22/10/43	

Date 22nd. October 194 3   Signature W. G. Grey major
                                           * President or Member of the Board

Date 194   Signature
                                           * President or Member of the Board

Date 194   Signature
                                           * President or Member of the Board

Date 194   Signature
                                           * President or Member of the Board

Date 194   Signature
                                           * President or Member of the Board

PART II. I certify that (Rank) L/Cpl. (Name and initials) SHERIDAN.P.H.

of 'A' ~~Battery~~ 55th. Kent ~~Regiment~~ HOME GUARD, having duly passed
        Company   Battalion
the Proficiency tests detailed above in accordance with the pamphlet and is hereby authorized to wear the Proficiency Badge, as laid down in Regulations for the Home Guard, Vol. 1, 1942, para. 4

Date [stamp: 55TH BATTALION HOME GUARD - 1 NOV 1943]   Signature A. Hooper Lt Col
                                        Commanding 55th. Kent Bn.   H.G.

PART III. If the holder joins ~~H.M. Forces~~, his Company or equivalent Commander will record below any particulars which he considers useful in assessing the man's value on arrival at the T.E., P.T.C., R.T.C., e.g. service, rank, duties on which employed, power of leadership, etc.

Date 194   Signature
* Delete where not applicable.   O.C.

6. 1943

"A few shells failed to explode and fell to earth . . ."

Beckenham Journal 23 January 1943

Air raids continued to affect school attendances. On 18 January they were very low because of a heavy air raid overnight. The Anti-Aircraft defences had been strengthened since the last heavy night raid of May 1941, so the populace was cheered by the sound of the immense fire-power of the guns. A few shells failed to explode, one falling in the back garden of 97 Kingsway. It exploded in front of a brick shelter, which it partially demolished, but the occupants were unhurt. Windows were blown in and tiles dislodged from the roofs. Two months later, Mrs. Phyllis Burton had a lucky escape when an unexploded shell crashed diagonally through her home at 92 Hayes Chase. The shell missed Phyllis Burton by inches but her leg was injured by fragments of plaster and although the house was in darkness and full of the acrid smell of explosives, she raced upstairs and snatched her seven month-old baby from its cot and made her way downstairs. By some miracle she and her baby escaped further injury even though part of the staircase had collapsed in the flight of the shell. Another shell destroyed the interior of a house in Chestnut Avenue, the only external sign – a broken window.

On 20 January Mrs. Margaret Edmeads was walking along Hawes Lane having just visited her sister at No. 65, when a German plane swooped low over the houses, low enough for the pilot to be seen to turn his head and laugh at Margaret Edmeads. Later she realised the plane was almost certainly returning from a raid on Catford where Sandhurst School had been hit and 38 children killed.

Surrender of German Army at Stalingrad. Everywhere the Germans are in retreat.

29 January   Tunisian border crossed by the 8th Army.

There were many patriotic fund-raising weeks. In March there was a Fancy Fair in the Toc H Hall for the Aid to China Fund. A dance and cabaret in the Lecture Hall, organised by Kent 82 detachment of the Red Cross, made £40 profit. The Red Cross Penny-a-Week Fund was flourishing and by the end of July, had paid for 2,951 Red Cross parcels for prisoners-of-war. There was a Wings for Victory Week in June. All sections of the community made strenuous efforts to make it a success. Hawes Down Junior School raised £1,368 11s. 7d. for National Savings, making a grand total to that date of £10,128 6s. 5d. The School also collected books for salvage and by mid-October had contributed 11,304 books to the campaign. Wickham Common School, no less enthusiastic, had, by the end of the War, raised over £12,000 for National Savings.

The list of prisoners-of-war in Japanese hands mounted steadily. The latest to be announced was LAC Hugh Mackinder of Hawes Lane and a bell-ringer at St. John's Church. He was soon followed by Gunner Leslie Jones and Bombardier Frank Keenor. Frank Crier, a 1st War soldier and now in the Home Guard, anxiously awaited news of his son Jack.

2 April   *Offensive opened by 1st Army in Northern Tunisia.*

The fighting in North-West Africa was followed at home with anxiety and great pride too. The award of an immediate DFM to LAC James Skingsley of Croft Avenue, for gallantry after an attack on the docks at Bizerta in March, was followed in May with the award of an MC to Lieutenant John Pickering of Sylvan Way, for services in Tunisia when associated with a Commando Unit.

At home there was a parade and pageant to mark the third anniversary of the formation of the Home Guard. The pageant re-created the development of the Force since the first days when the men were identified only by LDV armlets, and carried sporting guns and antiquated rifles. The programme included impressive demonstrations of how the training schedules had progressed, with specialist groups displaying their skills – in anti-gas procedures, signalling, Lewis bombs and bombing, automatic guns, Northover Projectors, Spigot Mortars, Browning machine-guns and Smith guns.

End of North-West Africa campaign when the Axis Forces in Tunisia surrender.

16 May   *RAF 'Dam-Buster' raid*

Pilot Officer Michael Fuller, one of the élite 617 Squadron, was killed in the raid on the Eder Dam on 17 May. The day before this historic raid, the Crier family received a telegram . . .

80

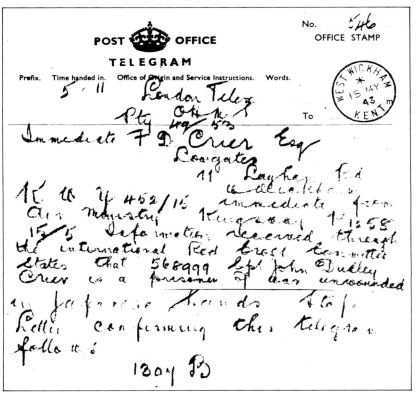

To be followed in July by . . .

調岡俘虜收容所俘虜郵便　IMPERIAL JAPANESE ARMY

July, 6, 1943.

My dear Parents.

I am interned in Fukuoka war prisoner' camp, Japan.

My health is excellent.

I am working for pay.

Remember me to Sallie.　My love to you all,

81

There are ten official Second War graves in St. John's churchyard. Eight are of members of the RAF, one of an ATS Private and one of a Home Guard, Corporal Arthur Chudley, aged 57, who collapsed and died on 6 June while on exercises in Rush Field Shaw at Keston.

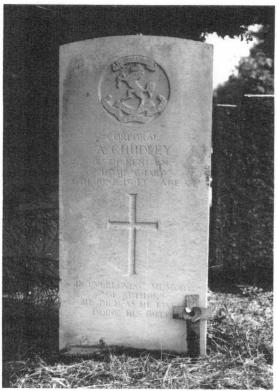

Grave of Corporal Arthur Chudley

Women of 46–50 called-up

The sporting scene was enlivened with various units of the Civil Defence and Home Guard entering into local combat. Beckenham Cricket Club took on a team from the 55 Kent Bn Home Guard, the latter a fairly strong team that included the future manager of the local Lloyds Bank, one Private Freddy Stiff. 'Stiffy' as he was known to his friends, was well-known in cricketing circles.

The West Wickham Residents Association, still active, drew the attention of Beckenham Borough Council to the overcrowding at Hawes Down Infants School and the fact that the school hall was being used as a classroom and a lunch room. It was also concerned about the number of Army lorries using Red Lodge Road, despite the notice exhibited at both ends of the road prohibiting its use by Army traffic. Another local concern was the state of the Glebe Way cutting – "It is high time the KCC did something to clear the foul and evil-smelling water."[60]

10 July	*Allies land in Sicily*
25 July	*Mussolini resigns and is arrested. He is rescued by German paratroops.*
3 September	*8th Army crosses to the Italian mainland.*
8 September	*Italy surrenders to the Allies.*

All sections of the community were now involved in the war effort and regular appeals were made to encourage young people. The Red Cross responded by organising a Youth Voluntary Aid Detachment, Kent 532, which was associated with Kent 82, an adult detachment. Younger children, eight years plus, were enrolled in a Cadet Unit. All these youngsters used the Toc H hall for their meetings later transferring to an empty shop (now Nottle's) in the High Streeet. The members of Kent 532 worked at the Day Nursery in Springfield; the Children's Heart Hospital; assisted the District Nurse on her rounds and, a very popular duty, on First Aid duty with the VADs of Kent 82 at the Odeon Cinema. Twenty of the girls who passed through Kent 532 went on to become State Registered Nurses, and one, Margaret Dawson (now Clark) became a Sister Tutor at Guy's Hospital. The Medical Officer to both Kent 82 and Kent 532 was Dr. G. de Hoghton Dawson who lived in Penge and who had had a distinguished career including service in the First World War, earning a DSO and MC in the process.

The Youth Organisations were augmented by a senior branch of Guiding – Rangers and Cadets – who met weekly at the Hawes Down School. The Scout movement was also expanding and G. H. Lakin-Hall was appointed District Commissioner, and Ken Nottle, District Scoutmaster. There were so many opportunities for young people to join youth organisations. There was purpose and pride in 'belonging'. The West Wickham and Beckenham Division of the St. John Ambulance Brigade was no exception. It won the Southern Area Shield for First Aid at its first attempt.

10 September	*Rome occupied by German troops.*
13 October	*Italy declares war on Germany.*

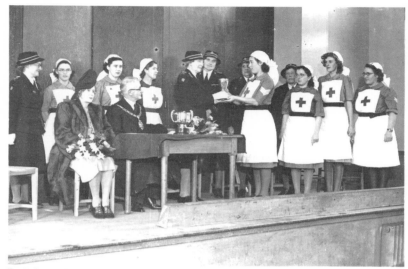

Red Cross Voluntary Aid Detachment 532

Red Cross Cadet Unit 4354

1943 was the year Bomber Command launched an all-out offensive against Germany. Casualties were heavy among the bomber crews. Confirmation came in November that Sergeant/Navigator John Wright had lost his life in air operations over Germany on 26 June 1943. Sergeant/Pilot Ronald Allcorn, a member of Emmanuel Church, was reported missing. Better news came of Sergeant/Rear-gunner John Saunders reported missing on October 2 – he was now a prisoner-of-war in Germany. A sailor, Eric Wharton, was a crew member of a fast motor launch which was shot up and sunk in the Dodecanese Islands in November. He was badly wounded in the head, arms and legs but was rescued by his attackers. After several spells in different hospitals, Eric Wharton ended up in a German hospital in Chemnitz. Another sailor, Bernard Pegley one of three brothers, was reported missing in December.

The fifth Christmas at war was a time of mourning and sad remembrances. How many more were there to come?

Grave of Sergeant Richard Durling   *Bert Durling*

Mobile Civil Defence Unit *Alice Abbott*

7. 1944

"Has a very funny rackety sound . . ."

Ida Watson

The so-called 'Little Blitz' began in London in early 1944. On 2 January Mrs. Dorothy Robbins, sitting in the back room of her home in Tiepigs Lane on the borders of West Wickham and Hayes, was killed by bombs falling at the rear of the house. Occupants of the neighbouring house, itself severely damaged, received only minor injuries as they had taken refuge in a shelter. Other bombs fell on the refuse dump on the other side of the road. As a consequence of this 'Little Blitz', sanction was obtained by the Beckenham Emergency Committee to distribute another 200 Morrison shelters.

Shells fell in Hawes Lane on 29 January, in Manor Road on 3–4 February and in Lime Tree Walk on 11–12 February. During a heavy barrage on 13 February a shell exploded outside 151 Pickhurst Rise on the pavement. It demolished a gate-post and broke innumerable windows, mostly on the opposite side of the road, but there were no casualties as most of the residents were in their shelters. Beckenham Road was 'shelled' on 18–19 February and was the recipient of incendiaries on Sunday 20 February, as were Springfield Gardens, Copse Avenue, Braemar Gardens and the High Street.

10 February   *Regional Commissioners of five Civil Defence Regions are warned about the threat from pilotless aircraft.*

An old boy of Hawes Down School, Sergeant/Pilot James Tilbury of The Avenue, was killed on active service in India. On another continent, Sergeant Richard Durling died on 13 February of wounds received in the fighting near the village of Caira on the slopes of Monte Castellino in Italy. Shortly to take a commission, Richard Durling before he enlisted, was a professional at Langley Park Golf Club. Another serviceman, Signaller R. Green was more fortunate – his name appeared on the prisoner-of-war list.

The 'Little Blitz' continued. On 22 March incendiaries fell in a field in Gates Green Road among parked Army vehicles and on a nearby house, 137 Gates Green Road. Three H.E. bombs fell in a row. The first demolished two empty houses and the second made a large crater in some allotments. The third bomb demolished The Dell in Hartfield Crescent where members of the Clouston family were sheltering under the kitchen table. Twenty-year-old Doris was so badly hurt that she died shortly after being taken out of the wreckage; her eighteen-year-old brother Ronald had a leg so severely injured that it had to be amputated; Mrs. Isobel Clouston received severe spinal injuries. Corporal John Clouston was granted compassionate leave to deal with the ensuing trauma. Within three months John was to become yet another casualty.

Warnings of more trouble to come were reiterated at a parade of 55 Kent Bn Home Guard when awards were presented. Brigadier Grahams spoke of two events likely to occur. One was the invasion of Europe which meant that the Home Guard would have to undertake extra protective measures. The second was German retaliation and that was why, the Brigadier said, that the Home Guard had recently been given Civil Defence training. How valuable that additional training was, would be demonstrated in the months to come.

Bomber Command maintained its offensive against Germany and the casualties continued to mount. Sergeant Cyril Williams, a wireless operator/air gunner, was killed in action and buried in St. John's churchyard on 19 April. Three DFCs were awarded to West Wickham men in June: Flight Lieutenant Leslie Berry, Pilot Officer Ronald Tuck and Flying Officer John Dymock. A sailor, Sub Lieutenant Noel Murray Simon, was Mentioned in Despatches for "undaunted courage . . . in the escort of convoys to and from North Russia . . ."[61] Two airmen made sombre news in July when their deaths were announced – Flight Lieutenant Ronald Andrews and Flying Officer Denis O'Callaghan.

| 4 June | *Rome occupied by Allied troops* |
| 6 June | *Invasion of Normandy* |

D-Day 6 June, the day long awaited and prepared for, had at last arrived. There was a price to pay. John Clouston and Raymond Hoer succumbed to wounds received in the fighting for Normandy.

On 13 June the V1 or Vergeltungswaffe (Revenge weapon), the pilotless aircraft advised to the Civil Defence Regional Commissioners, arrived and rained down death and destruction. The V1 flying-bombs, known as doodlebugs or buzz bombs, came intermittently by day and by night. There were many red-eyed people within a short space of time for the flying-bombs were already reaching Greater London at the rate of 73 a day. Audrey Thompson was on fire-watch duty at

Hawes Down School on the first night of the V1s. "We knew this was something different and very terrifying. The All Clear did not sound until well into the next day making it difficult to get home for breakfast and back to work. A young airman, walking back to Biggin Hill, was frightened and mystified by this new sound and came into our shelter . . ."[62]

On 16 June the Hawes Down Junior School Log Book read "Register not marked today owing to enemy action by pilotless aircraft." Ida Watson kept a record of that day and the enemy attack referred to in the School Log.

6.40 am   Another plane – has a very funny rackety sound – opened door and tried to see one and just as I shut it, big explosion which shook door and I thought something had hit it.
6.50 am   Another – sounded as if guns caught it.
6.52 am   Guns and another plane. No bombs. Approx two in quick succession.
7.00 am   Saw black smoke of one just over trees to left of us.
7.25 am   Guns – heard no bomb.
7.30 am   Plane – guns
7.35 am   Terrific guns and bomb. Few minutes later bomb burst overhead.
7.40 am   Guns
7.45 am   Another plane. Guns. 2 bombs exploded. Another lot.
8.15 am   Guns
8.20 am   Heard it coming down and blew my kitchen door open. Was Barwells and caught the place – woman brought out cut about. Also child cut in High Street.
9.20 am   All Clear
9.40 am   Warning again
10.05 am   Guns
10.20 am   Bomb
10.30 am   2 bombs; 2 bombs; Two or three minutes later – 1 bomb. Several warnings during morning.
1.15 pm   All clear noted.
1.45 pm   Alert
2.45 pm   All Clear
9.22 pm   Alert. Plane, guns and distant bomb.[63]

Later Ida Watson wrote up her notes about the bomb at Barwells.

"This new bomb which fell on nursery ground opposite Barwells [2 Links Road] did a terrible lot of damage. All shops in Station Road and High Street up to Sherwood Way lost their windows and all except three past Sherwood Way. Houses in Station Road were terrible wrecks: some almost inhabitable. Poor old Mr. Goodchild's (my gardener) house [10 Links Road] was just a shell . . . Mrs. Barber and I went to see both Goodchilds . . . and all we could find out about Mr. Goodchild for time being was he had gone into hospital. In evening I went down again and Mrs. Goodchild and her daughters and Mr. Felix were there and said poor Mr. Goodchild was unconscious, he had lost an eye, had a smashed arm and other injuries. He died the next morning. It has been a big blow to me as he was such a fine character and very kindly and helpful."[64]

Frank Goodchild was not the only casualty of that incident. Six members of the Hawes Down Heavy Rescue Party – Ernest Agate, Henry Bailey, Harold Browne, Frank Burton, Lawrence Lathwood and George Wingham – were killed when their lorry in which they were travelling was destroyed in Links Road when the bomb fell. The Rescue Party was returning from an incident at Tootswood Road where a Wardens' Post had been hit and three wardens killed. The Methodist minister, the Revd. Thomas Morrow, in his capacity as a Civil Defence Welfare Officer, had attended almost every serious incident in West Wickham. This particular incident was sadder than usual for Harold Browne was one of his congregation.

Mrs. Margaret Edmeads remembers that incident, as she was working in the Post Office in Station Road at the time. The Royal Observer Corps had ordered the Post Office to be closed and the staff to take cover. Margaret Edmeads was descending to the basement but the bomb exploded while her head was still above ground level. The resulting blast made her hair stand on end – "it was as straight as a die."[65]

There were no demarcation lines in the Civil Defence. Home Guards replaced windows, the NFS helped make houses waterproof. It was on one such occasion that Leading Fireman Frank Preston caught his first sight of a flying-bomb, in the act of placing a tarpaulin on the roof of a house in Manor Park Road. He thought it was an aeroplane on fire! Bomb damage repairs at St. Francis Church however, were postponed "until the many birds which truly make this a St. Francis Church, have hatched their young and taught them to fly."[66]

Soon after the flying-bomb campaign began, extra Mobile Medical Units were organised to respond to incidents as it had been found that some casualties died before reaching hosptial. Mrs. 'Buddy' Abbott was a member of one such unit. Hers consisted of a Medical Officer, three trained nurses and two partly-trained nurses and a driver. The ambulance was equipped with anaesthetics, dressings, splints etc., and could operate on the spot. The team worked a 24 hour shift system and 'Buddy' Abbott "will never forget the pluck of folk, their houses just rubble and the dreadful acrid smell".[67]

It was a dismal depressing time. Victory had seemed so near, peace

90

was beckoning and now this fearsome flying-bomb was dropping out of the skies over southern England. West Wickham was declared an evacuation area. Up till then the demarcation line of the Mid-Kent Railway line had operated, but this new menace changed all that. On 7 July a party of 46 children from Hawes Down Junior School left for Straithwaite, accompanied by Mr. Dixon and Joyce Draycott. Parties left on succeeding days for Doncaster, Barnsley and Leicester.

Audrey Thompson was with the Barnsley party. "We did not know of our destination until almost the end of the journey. On arrival we went to a centre where we were given a meal and met local dignitaries. The children were whisked away from us . . . We were worried by this, as were other teachers, and felt we could not face our parents not knowing where the children were or how they were faring. Eventually a coach was laid on and we went on a tour of the Yorkshire Moors, calling at all the village halls. We found our children, they had been put to bed but were pleased to see us. We said 'Good Night' to them and returned to Barnsley where Marion Hall and I were entertained overnight by the Chief of Police and his wife. We returned the next day."[68]

The parents of the children waved good-bye to their offspring who left in the buses assembled at the schools. Mrs. Dorothy Wingent was one of the mothers who trailed home sadly, quietly weeping, but she at least had a young baby to cuddle, care for and protect during this dangerous time. While returning from a visit to Shirley, Dorothy Wingent had just reached Bridle Way when a flying-bomb cut out overhead. She whisked her baby from out of his pram, placed him by a low brick wall and covered him with her body. Such was everyday life in West Wickham at this time.

On 8 July the *Beckenham Journal* printed a report about "inferred criticism that Civil Defence Rescue Squads had been last on the job, NFS first there . . ." The newspaper went on to refute this statement. "Civil Defence Units are despatched on orders from control when the locality of the occurrence has been reported by the Warden Service. The NFS now trained in rescue work is not so bound. Watchers sight the bomb bursts and vehicles are immediately despatched in that direction, frequently locating the incident before movement orders have been received by the Rescue Service." This was borne out by Oliver Woodman, then Senior Company Officer at Bromley who, in later years said that "each Station had a directional finder on a high tower and could observe, pinpoint and report an explosion to Headquarters. Three readings enabled a fast and accurate response."[69]

About 5.30 pm on 11 July a flying-bomb fell in the High Street, setting buses and cars on fire and damaging many shops. One person was killed and at least 20 injured. John Merigan was near the spot. "The White Hart . . . was the sight which I shall never forget. I was in the High Street near Woolworths when a dark shadow flew overhead – before I could discern what it was, the sky was full of black smoke just beyond where I was walking. I realised it was a close bomb and had the presence of mind to collect the First Aid equipment which was always kept at the Post. When I arrived at the scene of the target a car was stationary outside the White Hart, all ablaze. A young woman and her older parents were pulled out but not before the young woman was like a burnt rag doll and beyond medical help. We saved the other couple, at least to reach the hospital. The next thing was a bus had careered into the pond by the White Hart and we treated 38 people altogether. The driver and conductor were seriously injured. The ambulances took the rest to Beckenham Hospital." [70]

The following day, the 12th, a flying-bomb exploded in The Grove near No. 26. Ida Watson living in Boleyn Gardens, recorded the incident – "I caught blast in back bedroom, ceiling coming down, the other window in downstairs back room and the French door split and small windows in front downstairs covering carpet in glass, also small panes out of landing windows, front out, ceilings in front and back bedrooms and soot, also tiles. Barber's are worse still – not a room complete and all down Sherwood Way very bad. Two were killed and approx. 27 injured. 650 houses reported by Incident Officers as damaged." [71]

This incident also came within John Merigan's purview. He remembers one man being buried [72 year-old Tyler Norman was killed] and a woman trapped, and another woman rushing up and down The Grove with a dog in her arms. The trapped woman who was caught in the footings of the house, with a broken leg, was released by John Merigan. Her resourceful rescuer immobilised her broken leg with one of the floorboards. Two years later she returned to the Payantake shop where John Merigan was employed and renewed the acquaintance. Needless to say she was not immediately recognised.

Programmed as it is to fly a fixed distance on a pre-set course, the flying-bomb rapidly rebuts the comforting notion that lightning never strikes twice in the same place.

Bethlem Royal Hospital attracted seven flying-bombs to its grounds, costing the hospital in the process, its farm buildings, the use of five wards, its research unit and almost every door and window in several other buildings.

A flying-bomb fell in Addington Road behind Aldine's the news-agents. Ivy Crier had a lucky escape – she was sitting in a bus outside the shop when she and other passengers saw the bomb skimming the roof-tops. "As it cut out it fell behind Aldine's. Our bus shook and most of the glass shattered. I don't think anyone was killed. The ambulance took several away with shock and injuries. The poor driver was in such a state . . . he saw it coming right to him. I went on to work and not until I arrived there did I find out my head was slightly cut by flying glass, and bleeding."[72]

Pauline Parry (now James) was employed at a hairdresser's at 80 Croydon Road when the flying-bomb landed in Addington Road. "The glass in the front door had been blown out – it all seemed to be happening in slow motion – our dresses blown out and around us, like a ballerina's dress. Then we were on the floor – a few seconds had passed and one of our lady bosses was saying to us all – 'Come and have a sip of brandy for the shock'. So we all in turn had a little drop . . . and started to clear away the glass and mess."[73]

On 3 August a flying-bomb fell on Blake Recreation Ground. Others fell on Langley Park Golf Course, near Rouse Farm, Wickham Court Farm and Copse Avenue (in woodland). The bomb at Wickham Court Farm once more disturbed the clientèle at the Croydon Road hairdresser's. One lady "under one of the Perm machines with all the curlers, papers etc., was quite game to sit there while a doodle-bug was going over and take her chance. We girls were not so keen, for it was too close for comfort. So we prevailed upon the lady to come with us into our shelter, having managed to free her from the big Perm machine just in time to hear an enormous bang. The doodle-bug had landed in a field just below the church."[74]

The Civil Defence was hard pressed and air raid wardens were brought in from great distances to relieve those on duty. Those helping out in Wickham came from Wombwell in Yorkshire. Marines drafted in to help in the clearing-up operations were well received and billeted in local homes.

There were proposals at a very high level to induce Germany to shorten the range of the flying-bombs – the principal aiming point being Tower Bridge, but the shots were falling short. But even if the bombs could be deflected they would still land in built-up areas. As it was, most flying-bombs were landing in mainly residential areas south of the Thames. In the southern suburbs of London the mean point was Dulwich, and it was argued that if this could be put back further, they would do less damage and cause fewer casualties. At one stage in the discussions consideration was given to a scheme to induce the Germans to lower their aim by a further six miles so that

The fact that you have been addressing letters to Fukuoka need not worry you unduly, as we understand the Japanese authorities redirect letters to the correct camps.

We consider the general trend of your son's letter appears quite genuine. The more stilted sentences are similar to many others we have seen, but on the whole the letter is quite free. Zentsuji Camp in comparison with the majority of camps is one of the best, and the men do seem to have more licence in what they may say. Letters have now been received there by our men, and Red Cross supplies. The camp itself is situated on a fertile plain running up to pine covered hills on the island of Shikoku.

We hope these few details will help you to picture your son's surroundings in some small way. Thank you for sending us this further news concerning him.

Yours sincerely,

S.G.KING.

Controller.

Extract from a letter from the Red Cross to Frank Crier

94

the centre of the bombardment would be Shirley and West Wickham. Fortunately for West Wickham this particular scheme came to nought.

Letters from prisoners-of-war in Japanese hands had filtered through only slowly, but when they did arrive they brought great joy. At first only a stereotyped card was allowed. Jack Crier's first letter dated 20 November 1943 arrived at the end of June 1944. Jack's father Frank, wrote to the Red Cross and St. John War Organisation advising them of the contents of the letter and received a sympathetic response.

The invasion of Europe continued to take its toll. Signaller Royston Smith of Rose Cottages, injured in the fighting in Normandy, died on 5 August.

12 August   *Allies break out from Normandy.*

The new school year began with 21 present at Hawes Down Junior School. All the staff were present with the exception of Mr. Dixon who was escorting still more evacuees, this time to Huddersfield.

15 August   *Allied troops land in France from Mediterranean.*
25 August   *Liberation of Paris*
3 September   *Brussels liberated by British.*

As if the menace of the V1, the flying-bomb, had not been enough to bear, the V2, a long-range rocket carrying a large H.E. warhead, made its appearance. The first of them fell at 6.34 pm on 8 September at Chiswick. The double bang – the sound of the impact followed by, a split second after, the sonic boom as the rocket re-entered the earth's atmosphere – soon became the trademark of the rocket. Two more landed in the next two days and a fourth arrived on 11 September at Chelsfield. It made a spectacular explosion as it hit a tree.

It was Government policy initially, to impose press silence to prevent Germany from discovering where the rockets had landed. An incredulous populace was told by local authorities that the explosions were caused by gas mains, ammunition wagons and delayed-action bombs. It was not until 10 November that Prime Minister Winston Churchill revealed to the House of Commons the news of the long-range rocket.

No rockets fell on West Wickham, but they did fall in neighbouring districts and the sound of the explosions was heard at unnerving intervals. By early November V2s were landing at the rate of 30 a week. More than 200 had reached England by late November and over half reached the London area.

Among the casualties of service personnel was eighteen-year-old Betty Coppin of the ATS, who was killed by enemy shell-fire while on service at Dover. She was buried in St. John's churchyard.

Corporal Cyril Burnet of Coney Hill Road was shot by a sniper in Belgium while serving with the Sherwood Rangers. Pickhurst Rise mourned the loss of Sapper Rupert Heywood in France.

17–26 September   Battle of Arnhem
30 September   Calais surrenders to Canadian Forces.

With the cessation of continuous alerts, and flying-bomb attacks tailing off, most evacuees returned, and by the end of October the school rolls were almost back to normal. Young Rodney Wingent came home, a stranger to his two-year-old brother. Met by his parents, young Rodney was absolutely filthy having been on a train most of the day. He had grown out of his clothes with his wrists showing from his coat sleeves. While the Wingent family waited for a train home, an American G.I. gave a banana to Rodney's little brother who promptly tried to eat the skin. Bananas were an unknown fruit to wartime children.

14 October   Athens entered by British Forces.

On 5 November 'A' Company 55 Kent Bn Home Guard held a parade at the War Memorial when wreaths were laid in memory of comrades who had passed on. Other wreaths were laid by Sister Cherrill on behalf of the VADs of Kent 82 and Kent 532, and by the WVS. Later that month 'A' Company gathered with the rest of the Battalion for the Stand Down Parade. It began with a short service at the Odeon after which the men were addressed by the Battalion Commander, Lieutenant Colonel A. F. Hooper, who spoke of the 2,726 men who had served in the Battalion. After this ceremony the officers and men formed up in Station Road and adjacent roads and marched along to the saluting base at the junction of Beckenham Road and South Eden Park Road, opposite Justin Hall. They then dispersed on reaching Monks Orchard Road. That was not the end of the local Home Guard. Bonds of friendship forged out of adversity were to endure through an Old Comrades Association. More of that later.

Among other Stand Down Parades and Review Parades was that of firewomen, by the Queen at the London Regional Fire Headquarters. West Wickham Fire Station sent Gladys Williams, 'Red Willie', as its representative.

There was the problem of war-damaged houses. A Scottish repair worker lodging at 25 Links Road, was charged with stealing a bag of plaster from his employers the Ministry of Works, and defrauding them of twelve shillings. It seems that some unscrupulous house-holders were approaching war-damage repair men to undertake extra

96

In the years when our Country
was in mortal danger

Phillip Henry Hatton SHERIDAN

who served 25th May 1940 - 31st Dec 1944

gave generously of his time and

powers to make himself ready

for her defence by force of arms

and with his life if need be.

George R.I.

THE HOME GUARD

repairs for them in return for good tips. In this instance a Links Road householder had entered into a private contract with the Scot to plaster a ceiling and he had done the work in the time he was earning wages. The luckless Scot was fined £10.

It was not surprising that householders were opportunists in getting their houses put back in good order. The scale of war damage to houses was horrendous and inevitably there were complaints both about the speed of repair work and the quality of the labour force, mostly imported from elsewhere. Twenty workmen from the North of England, staying in a hotel in Earls Court, were arrested in West Wickham for stealing coal, but the prosecution failed for lack of evidence. Looting of damaged and unoccupied premises in the district was rife; it was no wonder that there was agitation to remedy the situation. The Women's branch of the West Wickham Constitutional Association passed a resolution urging "the employment of competitive builders, preferably local, on bomb damage repairs now and that these builders be permitted to undertake building immediately after the cessation of hostilities." [75]

Local builders were subsequently employed but still there were grumbles. One anonymous correspondent wrote to the *Beckenham Journal* giving details of work schedules and the number and length of tea breaks taken at a site office in Links Road.

There was an acute shortage of miners, so the then Minister of Labour, Ernest Bevin, had dreamed up a scheme in 1943 whereby one in every ten men called-up, was directed to the mines. Richard Dawes of Harvest Bank Road and Paul Driver and Wallie Kemp, members of the Hawes Lane Methodist Church, drew short straws as 'Bevin Boys'.

16 December   *German offensive in the Ardennes*

For most people the sixth wartime Christmas passed off quietly with Christmas card frost transforming the outdoor scene until it became blanketed out in fog. The weather was totally irrelevant to the Crier family for on Christmas Day the postwoman delivered a letter from son Jack:

". . . I was 25 four days ago and it seemed ages since I was merely 20 and still in England. However I always think of what a lot I have to which to look forward . . . There isn't much to say about life here, even if we were allowed to. It's mainly the old formula for existence: Work, Food and Sleep; very little else. We have received on an average one Red Cross parcel every three or four months and we all look forward to the time when we can receive a parcel from home . . . The Red Cross parcels put a little tone to rice and vegetables . . . I've often thought of what I'll do when I get back home and sometimes think I will take a holiday somewhere quiet and recuperate, depending entirely on whether we suffer any after effect from this diet . . .''

Jack Crier was able to celebrate the following Christmas in the loving secure company of his family.

Jack Crier after the War *Ivy Crier*

Post-war reunion of 3 Platoon 'A' Company 55 Kent Bn Home Guard. Back row L – R: H. Palmer, M. Smale, S. Savage, E. Rice, W. Kerridge, E. Agutter, R. Kerridge, E. Peckham, R. Child, (?), R. Wright, H. Sheridan, (?), (?), E. Pullen. Middle row L – R: H. Rickard, D. Sara, (?), A. Miller, (?), C. Harper, (?), A. Whichelow, H. Thompson, E. Rees, (?), (?), A. Silverton. Front row L – R: B. Bryer, C. Whitfield, K. Flin, A. Davie, R. Bounsell, (?), L. Webber, L. Walker, S. Snazell, T. Indge *Arthur Davie*

8. *1945*

"I'm coming home!"
Jack Crier

The last winter of the War was a severe one, aggravated by war weariness. Victory was so near but yet so far away. For 21-year-old Sergeant/Pilot Peter Charman, whose plane was badly damaged over Burma, the War was over. He had ordered his crew to bale out but left it too late to save himself. Peter Charman, still at school when war broke out, was buried in Burma.

Relatives of Japanese prisoners-of-war worried and waited. Mrs. Catherine Bellringer received a postcard from her son Arthur. Mrs. Eddie Day heard from her husband, a former centre-forward with West Wickham Football Club.

Mention has already been made of the Home Guards' wish to continue their friendships. Unique bonds of comradeship were forged during the War in all branches of the Civil Defence and Armed Forces. Experiences had been shared that could not be spoken of to those not party to them. As a result, various Old Comrades Associations came into being, providing outlets for the wish to continue in association with one another. One such was the West Wickham Home Guard Association which was formed out of 'A' and 'B' companies of the 55th Kent Bn.

The Home Guard during its existence had discovered collective performing talents which came to fruition with an original pantomime 'Babes in the Wood', presented at the Coney Hall in January 1945. Written and produced by Bernal Bennett and Kenneth Flin, it was a resounding success.

The West Wickham Home Guard Association continued to produce an annual pantomime for many years, eventually becoming the West Wickham Pantomime Society. There were other social occasions in rented premises at the top end of The Grove, previously used by the West Wickham Hard Courts Tennis Club – now flattened and developed for housing. The ghosts of the past were captured on film by Gerry Vinall, who filmed the final parade of the Home Guard, and events at the club premises in The Grove.

16 January	Germany Ardennes offensive is finally defeated.
20 January	Russian troops enter Germany
4 February	Belgium finally liberated.

The 'Stand Downs' continued. Now it was the turn of the former AFS part-timers who had not only fought fires, but assisted in the general tidying-up of houses. Some 2,000 man-hours had been given to removing furniture, tiling and sheeting of roofs, repairing doors and locks and general first-aid repairs. The AFS men celebrated their transfer to the Reserve with a dinner at the Regal ballroom in Beckenham. An annual dinner begun before the War continued for many years, and always printed on the back of the dinner card were the names of colleagues killed in 1941.

NATIONAL FIRE SERVICE

CERTIFICATE OF SERVICE

Name (*in full*) .... FR JN ⬤ LN SON. ....

National Fire Service No. ..501.7?3....   *Date of discharge* ....20.3.45. ....

Rank on discharge .... Leading Firsm.n. ....

Cause of discharge .... Reduction of estblishmnt. ....

	WITH LOCAL AUTHORITY FIRE BRIGADE	WITH NATIONAL FIRE SERVICE
WHOLE-TIME SERVICE	*from* ———/———	*from* ———/———
	to ———————	*to* ———————
PART-TIME SERVICE	*from* 4.5.39. ———	*from* 18.8.41. ———
	to 17.3.41. ———	*to* 20.8.45. ———

.............20.8.19.45.   *Fire Force Commander.*

There were more celebrations in Highfield Drive when AB Eric Wharton was repatriated in March. He had made a good recovery from most of his injuries but would still need hospital treatment for a leg wound. There were no celebrations for the family of Flight Sergeant Frank Russell killed in action on 25 February. He now rests with other members of the RAF in St. John's churchyard.

March was to prove the final month of aerial bombardment from Germany. The last rocket landed at 4.37 pm on 61 and 63 Kynaston Road, Orpington on 27 March. The last flying-bomb fell on 29 March.

British and American troops cross the Rhine.

In April about 40 people attended a meeting in the Lecture Hall for the purpose of forming a branch of the British Legion. Captain Mason took the chair and following a speech from Major W. R. Birrell MC from Legion Headquarters, a formal resolution was passed to form a branch in West Wickham. Captain D'Eath was appointed secretary and Frank Padfield the treasurer. While the British Legion was being formed, the Toc H was struggling to re-establish itself. Of the seven units in the Spring Park district, only the Coney Hall Branch had been able to meet regularly during the War.

26 April	*Russian and American Forces link up on the Elbe near Torgau.*
28 April	*Death of Mussolini, executed by Italian partisans.*
29 April	*Surrender of German Armies in Italy and Austria.*
1 May	*Death of Hitler by suicide, announced by Germany.*
7 May	*Unconditional surrender of all German fighting forces.*
8 May	*Victory in Europe Day – VE Day*

May 8 and 9 were celebrated by most with great jubilation. The children were made the focal point of many parties. There were street parties galore and many bonfires. All the churches joined in a Thanksgiving Service in St. Francis Church and there were special Thanksgiving Services at St. Francis and Emmanuel Churches. These special services were attended by representatives from the WVS, Women's Institute, ARP wardens, Royal Observer Corps, 1st West Wickham Boy Scouts, Wolf Cubs, Chamber of Commerce, Rotary Club, NFS, West Wickham Youth Club, Youth Hostels Association, British Red Cross Society, 'A' and 'B' Companies and the Mobile Column of the 55 Kent Bn Home Guard.

'Stand Downs' continued. 'C' Depot of the Civil Defence at Hawes Lane held a farewell party; there was a 'Stand Down' parade of the Civil Defence in Croydon Road Recreation Ground; the Royal Observer Corps held a dance at the Shirley Poppy Hotel. The West

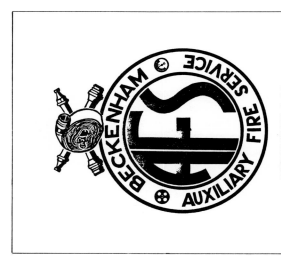

BECKENHAM A.F.S.

DINNER

THE PUBLIC HALL · BECKENHAM
OCTOBER 1st, 1938

Chairman - T. Gordon Smith, Esq.

Wickham Pig Club was formally closed at a social evening when it was announced that a total of 1,000 guineas had been raised for the Red Cross Prisoner-of-War Fund. The Spring Park Rabbit Club was wound up. A WVS Club opened in the Toc H Hall with the aim of keeping members of the WVS in touch with one another.

The prisoners-of-war returned in increasing numbers. The family at 21 Pickhurst Rise and its neighbours welcomed home Sergeant John Hawes who had spent five long years in a German camp. Another long-term prisoner was Corporal Gerald Parsons. He had spent three years imprisoned in Poland from whence he escaped via Danzig on a Swedish cargo boat. He was recaptured before reaching Sweden. Another escape attempt failed and a third resulted in him being sent to Bavaria.

The European War was won but there was still a war being fought in the Far East. Flight Sergeant/Observer Donald Rose, better known as 'Bud', who lived in the School House in Hawes Lane, was killed in action on an operation ten miles from Bengal.

15 July	*A pre-war standard of street lighting comes into effect in southern England.*
26 July	*Labour victory in General Election.*
6 August	*Atomic bomb dropped on Hiroshima.*
9 August	*Atomic bomb dropped on Nagasaki.*
14 August	*Japan surrenders*
	"From 15 August all work of war damage repair which involves bringing houses beyond the second stage of tolerably comfortable, that is, mostly work of redecoration – will be held in abeyance until winter weather indicates a return to such purely inside work, and all labour is to be concentrated in badly-damaged unoccupied houses." [76]
15 August	*Victory over Japan Day celebrated – VJ Day.*

By 9 am on 15 August the High Street was busy as hundreds of shoppers tried to do their shopping in the short time the shops would be open. There were flags and bunting everywhere. There were Victory Parties, genuine ones this time, marking the end of all hostilities. There were Victory Dances, Children's Sports and the inevitable bonfires. There was a Victory Parade in London, watched on television by at least one household in West Wickham. Tom Wingent was in a reserved occupation as a glass-blower and as such worked on highly secret work at Crystal Palace making cathode ray tubes. As a consequence he possessed one of the first television sets and was able to offer hospitality on this very special day to a host of his neighbours in Manor Park Road.

105

Those who had cause to mourn kept themselves to themselves and thought about what might have been and how to face a world at peace without partners and providers.

On 18 August a Canadian airman, Murray Fonsar, married Ella Little of Birch Tree Avenue, in St. John's Church. Canada received from West Wickham at least 44 brides and 27 babies, most of whom were baptised in St. John's Church.

Uppermost in a great many minds was the fate of prisoners-of-war in Japanese hands, who had suffered great privations and cruelty at the hands of their captors. Cables began to arrive from the prisoners announcing their release and their whereabouts. Many of them needed medical treatment and so had to spend time recuperating before undertaking the long journey home. Letters arrived, read and re-read. Tears were shed. Nothing else mattered but that they were safe. 29 September 1945 was a red letter day for the Crier family:

"Dear Folks,

The day has at last arrived, and what a day. We left the old POW camp feeling absolutely marvellous. The mere thought of being free has put pounds on every one of us. We had listened to, and watched trains go by with longing in our hearts, for such a long time and at last the rattle bash sounded from under our seats. We had been situated in the centre of the Inland Sea called Mukaishico and travelled for twenty odd hours up to Yokohama by train where the Yanks turned out in force to meet us. We pulled into the strains of 'Roll out the Barrel' and other tunes, some of which were strange to us; and then General Eichinpergor [sic] himself shook hands with everyone of the five hundred who detrained there. My heart was too full for words. I could easily have cried I was that happy. And the girls ! ! ! What a pleasure to see good lookers again. No black hair, black slanted eyes or stunted stature. We were rushed to the harbour, given a meal, bath, medical examination – re-kitted with new clothes and toilet necessities and shipped to a bit of Blighty's floating soil. There were no pangs of parting when the harbour side slid away to the rear. No Sir! and when we move off I'll get a real kick watching Japan disappear over the horizon . . . *I'm coming home!*

Love, Jack"

News coming out of the Far East was not always so joyful. Councillor Mrs. Catherine Bellringer who had worked so hard for the Red Cross Prisoner-of-War Fund and the Next of Kin Club in the belief that her son Arthur was a prisoner-of-war in Thailand, received the shattering news that he had been shot and killed whilst attempting to escape. Fate dealt many cruel blows in the War – this certainly was one such.

So many wrongs had to be righted in this post-war period – wounded to be healed; shattered minds to find balm; families to learn to live together again. Having won the war, the peace had its problems too. Among those problems was that of the desperate housing shortage. Land fronting the High Street and The Alders was compulsorily acquired for five temporary prefabricated bungalows, soon to be nicknamed 'prefabs'. An irritant rather than a problem were the various anti-tank concrete blocks dotted around the landscape. The Borough Council entered into negotiations with the relevant Government department when "out of the blue a firm of contractors started to blow the blocks up with gelignite and not being too careful about it." [77]

The first peace-time Christmas was a time of mixed emotions. There was on one hand great happiness for those whose families had survived more or less intact, but for those bereaved families, especially those who had lost the breadwinner, there was the realisation that the outlook for the immediate future was bleak. It was not always the case that it was a serviceman who had been killed, for the 'People's War' had claimed 41 civilians and 20 Civil Defence personnel, almost on a par with at least 62 deaths in the Armed Forces. [78]

British Legion Standard outside The Odeon *Beckenham Journal*

UXB in Pickhurst Rise 1946 *Beckenham Journal*

Civil Defence Memorial *Joyce Walker*

9. *After the War*

"During the play . . . the fitness of some of the older players who had been serving with the Forces stood them in very good stead . . ."

Beckenham Journal 19 January 1946

Many sports had lapsed during the War. Of the West Wickham Football Club's 51 members, 49 had served in the Forces, five of whom were killed. After a meeting attended by 25 members and other enthusiasts it was decided to re-form a team. Eight members of the 1st XI were available and they with three others beat the Old Balgowans 3–2 a fortnight later. The affairs of the Club were temporarily left in the capable hands of Messrs Miller, Bounsall and Purkiss. The soccer section of the Wickham Park Sports Club was revived the following September.

As the threads of peace-time were being drawn together there were still those in the community hoping against hope that their missing loved-ones were still alive. Ernest Gardner abandoned all hope in June with an announcement in the *Beckenham Journal* – "Previously reported missing now presumed dead killed in action in Singapore on or about February 13th 1942, Gunner Leonard V. Gardner 2/6th Heavy AA Battery RA, aged 20. Elder son of E. V. Gardner 28 Stambourne Way."

A 500lb unexploded bomb that had lain buried in waste ground at the back of Pickhurst Rise since October 1940, was defused by the Royal Engineers. Edwin Samuel, a local warden at Post 55 had a long memory and fortunately had voiced his suspicions to the police. The search began in July in the area behind 154 and 156 Pickhurst Rise, accessible through a passage-way, itself half-filled with concrete defence blocks. A shaft was sunk some 50 yards behind the houses where the bomb was found. The occupants of Nos. 132–178 were advised to keep to the front of their houses while the defusing took place.

While one legacy of the War was being disposed of, another happier one was taken on board when the British Legion Standard was dedicated in St. John's Church in September. It was followed by a march from Coney Hall Recreation Ground to the Odeon Cinema in Station Road where the mayor of Beckenham took the salute. It was the proud lot of Leslie Smith to be the Standard Bearer supported by Bert Uzzell and Bill Dawson.

A sad but fitting ceremony was the unveiling in Beckenham Cemetery of a memorial to the members of the Beckenham Civil Defence killed while on duty. It included the names of the Hawes Down Heavy Rescue Squad killed in Links Road in 1944. A further inscription was added to Wickham's War Memorial "in remembrance of those men and women who gave their lives 1939–1945." The Memorial Board in St. John's Church was enlarged to accommodate and remember another generation.

And as the final farewells were said and the opportunities presenting themselves for friendships and fresh starts in the community were taken up, post-war Britain was struggling to get into its stride. It was to be a long haul.

Remembrance Day 1988 *Bert Durling*

10. *Honours and Awards*

Corporal Jack Allison 2573060 RCS
Awarded the MM. " . . . for operations in North Africa."
London Gazette 23 September 1943

"On 18th March, 1943 near NEFSA (Tunisia, sheet 10) during a readjustment of positions by 2nd Battalion, The Parachute Regiment, this N.C.O. was in charge of the Brigade Wireless Set and crew. Owing to the intense enemy fire it became necessary to move along a river bed in order to obtain cover and protection of the steep banks. In spite of this, many casualties were suffered, including a Signalman of Cpl Allison's crew who was severely wounded. Without hesitation and under heavy fire he went to the wounded man's aid and after several attempts succeeded in getting him out of the river to a nearby gully where he dressed the wounds. Disregarding his personal safety he went through intense fire and brought back a stretcher party and assisted to return the wounded man safely to our lines.

By his undaunted courage he undoubtedly saved the life of one of his crew."
Ministry of Defence 23 December 1982

Chief Petty Officer Charles G. N. Anscomb Ch/J 107352 HMS Parthian
Awarded the DSM July 1940 "for courage and enterprise and devotion to duty in successful submarine patrols."
London Gazette September 1940
Mentioned in Despatches October 1941

Sergeant Leonard A. Ball Chief Instructor Home Guard Bombing School
Awarded the Home Guard Certificate of Good Service
Beckenham Journal 18 September 1943

Sergeant J. H. Bennett 'B' Company 55 Kent Bn Home Guard
Awarded the Home Guard Certificate of Good Service
Beckenham Journal 24 February 1945

Sub Lieutenant Geoffrey Benton RNVR

Mentioned in Despatches

Bromley Mercury 6 April 1945

Flight Lieutenant Leslie F. Berry RAFVR 622 Squadron

Mentioned in Despatches January 1942

Awarded the DFC having ". . . completed large number of operational sorties, including several against Berlin. On two occasions his aircraft has been attacked by an enemy fighter, each time his accurate return fire has probably caused the destruction of the enemy. A courageous, determined and efficient air gunner, this officer has also proved an excellent squadron gunnery leader."

Beckenham Journal 1 June 1944

Commander Julian W. Best RNR

Awarded the DSO for "taking in a destroyer and evacuating troops under fire in the evacuation from Greece. Senior Naval Officer in nearly every occupied port in succession from Mersa Matruh to Tripoli in the Libya Campaign, King's Harbour-master at Brindisi."

Bromley Mercury 25 August 1944

Three times Mentioned in Despatches.

Richard J. Border

Appointed MBE "for services rendered while engaged in communication work in connection with Civil Defence Services."

Bromley Mercury 8 January 1943

Pilot Officer John S. Campbell RAFVR 578 Squadron

Awarded the DFC. ". . . has participated in many operational sorties including attacks against such major targets as Karlsruhe, Kiel and Sterkrade. He has proved himself to be a skilful and courageous air gunner. By his untiring vigilance and excellent tactics he has materially assisted his Captain to outwit enemy fighters on three separate occasions. His fortitude and devotion to duty have been most praiseworthy. When operating against Bottrop in July 1944 his oxygen supply failed for four minutes at 20,000 feet. Despite his physical suffering, P/O Campbell refused to leave his turret and maintained his close watchfulness."

Beckenham Advertiser 1 March 1945

Colonel Francis Chamberlain London District Home Guard. Commander 'P' Zone

Appointed CBE (Military Division)
Beckenham Advertiser 8 January 1942

Pilot Officer Alfred R. Chandler RAFVR 635 Squadron

Awarded the DFC ". . . has completed 70 Pathfinder missions."
Beckenham Advertiser 2 June 1945

Lance Corporal Robert Clarke Rifle Brigade (Prince Consort's Own)

Awarded the MM. ". . . in recognition of gallant and distinguished services in the Middle East."
Bromley Mercury 11 June 1943

Flying Officer George B. Colbourn RAFVR 98 Squadron

Awarded the DFC. ". . . has completed two tours of operational duty. Throughout he has displayed skill and determination of the highest order. He has participated in many important missions against heavily defended targets and has set an excellent example of cheerful confidence and devotion to duty at all times."
Beckenham Advertiser 15 February 1945

Councillor John Collett Royal Observer Corps

Awarded the BEM (Civil Division) for meritorious services.
Beckenham Journal 21 June 1941

Lieutenant (E) Ian H. Cowie RNR

Mentioned in Despatches "for outstanding skill, determination and despatch in carrying out minesweeping operations frequently under fire, off the East coast of Italy."
Beckenham Journal 5 May 1945

Wing Commander G. A. Dennis RAF Intelligence Branch

Appointed OBE (Military Division)
Beckenham Advertiser 1 February 1945

Lieutenant John P. Dill 2184 New Zealand Artillery

Mentioned in Despatches
Commonwealth War Graves Commission

Sergeant Frederick W. Douglas 923456 RAF 78 Squadron

Awarded the DFM for consistently displaying the greatest coolness and devotion to duty.

London Gazette 18 May 1943

Flight Lieutenant John D. Dunbar 130943

Awarded the DFC. "Since January 1945 this officer has been in charge of a corps detachment to a group communication squadron and has accomplished all his duties with skill and initiative. During this period he has piloted many very important persons on visits, inspections and reconnaissances of forward troops. In addition to Flight Lieutenant Dunbar's being attached to the forward troops, he has completed several operations of a hazardous nature. On two occasions this officer has landed under enemy artillery and small arms fire in order to complete his mission and in May 1945, he led a flight of four aircraft behind the enemy lines to bring out survivors of a crashed aircraft. At all times Flight Lieutenant Dunbar has displayed courage and determination of a high order.

Beckenham Journal 24 February 1945

Flying Officer John W. Dymock RAFVR 78 Squadron

Awarded the DFC for ". . . displaying high skill, fortitude and devotion to duty in many successful operations against the enemy."

Beckenham Journal 10 June 1944

Lieutenant Eric F. J. Eames RA

Awarded the MC for gallantry in action at Malta.

Kentish Times 20 March 1943

Lance Sergeant Norman E. Fitter 'A' Company 3 Platoon 55 Kent Bn Home Guard

Awarded the Home Guard Certificate of Good Service

Beckenham Journal 12 February 1944

Ernest A. Garland

Awarded King's Commendation

"For his gallantry during the heavy bombing of London's docks in September . . . has been commended by the King . . . On occasion of enemy attack on the Surrey Commercial Docks on September 7th and 8th 1940."

London Gazette 24 January 1941

Flying Officer Kenneth T. Garner RAF

Awarded the American Air Medal. "This officer, a pilot of a glider-towing aircraft participated in sorties during the airborne operations at Arnhem. His keenness, courage and determination contributed materially to the success of these operations."

Beckenham Journal 28 April 1945

Sergeant Kenneth H. Gray Mobile Platoon 55 Kent Bn Home Guard

Awarded the Home Guard Certificate of Good Service.

Beckenham Journal 24 February 1945

Lieutenant Sidney Goodchild RE

Mentioned in Despatches for bravery.

Beckenham Advertiser 18 November 1943

Seaman William A. Gritt RNR 17880A

Mentioned in Despatches

London Gazette 1 January 1944

Flying Officer Ross James 35 Squadron

Awarded the DFC. ". . . has taken part in between 20 and 30 raids over Germany. The objectives included Berlin. He has recently flown Flying Fortresses across the Atlantic . . ."

Beckenham Advertiser 28 August 1941

Flight Sergeant Kenneth F. Judd RAFVR 35 Squadron

Awarded the DFM "for gallantry and devotion to duty in the execution of air operations against the enemy."

Beckenham Journal 6 October 1945

Sergeant L. A. Leach 'A' Company 3 Platoon 55 Kent Bn Home Guard

Awarded the Home Guard Certificate of Good Service

Beckenham Journal 24 February 1945

Able Seaman Ronald Lilly RN

Awarded the Croix de Guerre following service with the Free French Navy. "A radar operator of MTB 90 he took part in twenty operations of war off the coast of France during eight months and on the night of May 19, 1944, in the course of action against four enemy ships before the island of Jersey, he showed extraordinary coolness despite very atmospheric conditions and maintained radar service for 1½ hours, maintaining contact with the enemy ships and furnishing his Commanding Officer with efficient information up to the very moment of firing torpedoes."

Beckenham Advertiser 9 August 1945

Corporal George A. Mason RAC

Awarded the MM for gallantry and distinguished services in the Middle East.

London Gazette 24 February 1942

Flight Lieutenant Charles H. Mathewman RAFVR 109 Squadron

Awarded DFC and Bar.

London Gazette 6 June 1944 and 23 March 1945

Awarded the DSO. "Flight Lieutenant Mathewman is an officer who has rendered very gallant and efficient service as a navigator. He has completed three tours of operational duty and by his courage and fearlessness has earned the admiration of all in the squadron. By his sound knowledge of the equipment in use and by his very reliable navigation he has set a fine example. Many of his recent missions have been completed in the role of target marker on tactical targets – an arduous task which he has accomplished with fine resuls.'

Beckenham Journal 29 September 1945

Lance Bombardier Francis H. B. Meads RA

Awarded the MM for services in Italy. "L/Bdr Meads has been in charge for several months of an Advanced Post of the Sound-Ranging Troop of 56th Observation Battery. During the period 19th August to 20th December 1944, while the Battery was in action under Command 4th US Corps and 6th South African Armoured Division, he set a particularly outstanding example of leadership and devotion to duty. When the Troop was deployed south of Oisa, his post was heavily shelled and mortared for long periods, but he kept it in action, and the morale of his men high, even when the infantry had retired owing to the heavy shelling, thereby making possible the continued location of hostile batteries. This fine example was continued on later bases under similar conditions on the Serchio, at Pistola, where his task was made more difficult by frequent infiltration of enemy patrols, and at Rioveggio, south of Bologna. Throughout, the efficiency of his post was of the highest standard, and the morale of his men remained equally high. Without relief, he maintained this standard by his fine leadership and unshaken determination."

Beckenham Journal 4 August 1945

Corporal Douglas W. Micklewright RF

Awarded the DCM for services on the Italian front. "On 14th September 1944 Cpl Micklewright was commanding the leading section of his platoon during a battalion attack. He advanced rapidly across country, drove the enemy from some houses. From there he led a dash to some houses and caught a party of Germans as they were emerging from their shelters. The enemy surrendered and Cpl Micklewright pushed on to the crest where he came under small arms fire from the area of a house on the right flank.

Undaunted by the hail of bullets he led his section in a quick assault down the hill to the enemy positions. The slit trenches forward of the house were over-run and the enemy surrendered. Jumping over the surrounding fence, Cpl Micklewright dashed round the side of the house, where he was met by a burst of machine-gun fire and wounded. He threw a grenade through a window and again tried to enter the house, but was again badly wounded in the head by a mortar bomb. By this time every member of his section had been killed or wounded, and Cpl Micklewright ordered the remnants to withdraw under covering fire from his tommy gun. Not until every member of his section was safely under cover did Cpl Micklewright himself withdraw. He was wounded a third time by fire from an enemy tank.

Although by the time he reached company headquarters on a stretcher he was very weak from loss of blood and only semi-conscious, he accurately described the position of three enemy positions which were then knocked out by artillery fire.

Throughout this action Cpl Micklewright showed superb personal courage and dash, and it was largely due to him and to his inspiring leadership, initiative and drive, that the company were able to capture and hold their objective.''

Beckenham Journal 7 April 1944

Captain J. R. Mitchell Mobile Platoon 55 Kent Bn Home Guard

Awarded the Home Guard Certificate of Good Service.

Beckenham Journal 24 February 1945

Sergeant Charles H. Mordy HQ Company 55 Kent Bn Home Guard

Awarded the Home Guard Certificate of Good Service

Beckenham Journal 24 February 1945

Company Sergeant Major Laurence Norris Intelligence Corps

Awarded the MM. "On August 4th this warrant officer accompanied the second in command of a special mission in Florence, designed to make contact with the Patriot Forces in the city and to act as liaison between these Forces and the Allied Military Forces during the battle. At all times with entire disregard for his personal danger he rendered invaluable assistance to the head of the mission in his dealings with the National Committee of Liberation.

On August 10th he accompanied the detachment to the northern banks of the river which at that time was in enemy hands and in conjunction with the Patriot Forces he was responsible for organising the defences of the Palaccio Vecchio area. He maintained contact with forward elements of the Patriots and was eventually shot in the leg by a sniper close to the Piazza Cavour on August 14th.

His great coolness and devotion to duty were an inspiration to the Patriot Forces with whom he worked so closely and he contributed much to the success of these forces in Florence."

Bromley Mercury 25 May 1945

Major N. A. Oakes RASC

Mentioned in Despatches in recognition of gallantry and distinguished service in NW Europe.

Beckenham Journal 24 August 1946

Flying Officer Henry C. S. Page 61 Squadron

Awarded the DFC. "Flying Officer Page took part in many bombing raids over Germany. In a raid over Hamburg his machine was damaged by anti-aircraft fire and ran into an electrical storm when nearing home."

Beckenham Journal 17 May 1941

Lieutenant John L. Pickering Reconnaissance Corps

Awarded the MC for services in Tunisia. "On February 26th 1943 Lt. Pickering's Squadron was operating on the high ground between Bouarad and Goubellat (Tunisia) in conjunction with a Commando Unit. Firing was heard from the direction of this unit's positions, and Lt. Pickering was sent with his troop to investigate and assist, if possible. On approaching the firing Lt. Pickering saw four German Mark III tanks attacking the Commando Headquarters. He immediately moved along the flank of the Commandos distracting the attention of the tanks and drawing their fire on to himself, thus enabling the Commando Headquarters to move into a wadi and re-organise. In so doing he handled his troop with such skill that he was able to extricate them with only the loss of one carrier which became bogged.

The following day in the same area, his troop was leading the advance when his two leading light reconnaissance cars were knocked out by German 88mm guns. Lt. Pickering crawled forward with a light machine-gun on the flank and killed the crew of one of the 88mm guns. The other gun having been put out of action by artillery fire, the advance was then able to continue.

Throughout the whole period Lt. Pickering's actions were of the highest order, his resourcefulness and disregard of danger, were an example to his troop and his devotion to duty on all occasions has been of the highest order.''

Beckenham Journal 29 May 1943

Lieutenant (Temp. Captain) Frederick J. Pinchen RASC

Appointed MBE (Military Division). "At Taranto on July 17 1944 an oil barge was re-fuelling an ocean tanker when fire broke out on the barge and spread up the pipe-line to the large ship and also on the surrounding water. The cargo of the tanker was in imminent danger of fire and exploding. In order to direct an effective jet of foam on the fire, Captain Pinchen jumped from the tanker jetty with a fire hose round his arm and swam in the burning sea to a position from which it was possible to bring the hose to play. He was aware that the tanker contained thousands of tons of aviation petrol and that fire was liable at any moment to reach this cargo. His most courageous action undertaken with complete disregard for his own safety, alone prevented a major disaster and saved the lives of others.''

Beckenham Journal 16 June 1945

Captain John Reading RCS

Appointed MBE (Military Division).

London Gazette 14 October 1943

Sub Lieutenant Noel Murray Simon RNVR

Mentioned in Despatches "for undaunted courage, skill and devotion to duty while serving in, or operating from HM Ships . . . in the escort of convoys to and from North Russia in the face of determined attacks by U-Boats.''

London Gazette 18 July 1944

Leading Aircraftman James A. Skingsley 142 Squadron

Awarded an immediate DFM. "One night in January 1943 S/L Booth, Sgt. Edwards and LAC Skingsley were Captain, Bomb Aimer and Acting Flight Engineer respectively of an aircraft which attacked the docks at Bizerta. Shortly after the bombs were released the aircraft was subjected to a series of attacks by an enemy fighter, sustaining much damage before the attacker was driven off. The starboard engine was hit and burst into flames, the hydraulic system rendered useless and the rear turret and other equipment damaged; in addition a portable oxygen bottle was set on fire. The aircraft began to lose height and the situation appeared hopeless. The Captain ordered his crew to prepare to abandon the aircraft. LAC Skingsley ignoring his parachute pack, however attempted to extinguish the flames from the oxygen bottle. Sgt. Edwards came to his assistance and together grasped the blazing bottle with their bare hands, carried it to the escape hatch and hurled it out. The fire in the engine and the main plane subsided and S/L Booth decided to attempt to fly the bomber home. All moveable equipment, including guns and ammunition, was jettisoned in an effort to maintain height. Although the aircraft was difficult to control, S/L Booth succeeded in flying it to base where he made a successful crash landing in the face of extremely harassing circumstances. These members . . . displayed courage and devotion to duty in keeping with the highest traditions of the RAF.''

London Gazette 19 March 1943

Corporal R. G. Smith HQ Staff 'P' Sector Home Guard

Awarded the Home Guard Certificate of Good Service.

Bromley Mercury 6 April 1945

Yeoman of Signals Sydney F. Stevens

Awarded the DSM in the King's Birthday Honours List 1944

Flight Lieutenant Edward H. Stringer RAFVR 50 Squadron

Awarded the DFC. ''. . . participated in attacks on many of the more important targets in Germany and by his accuracy has contributed materially to the successes obtained . . . throughout this officer has displayed great courage and devotion to duty.''

Beckenham Journal 23 January 1943

Corporal Frederick T. Thew 'A' Company 3 Platoon 55 Kent Bn Home Guard

Awarded the Home Guard Certificate of Good Service. ''On the night of 16 April 1941 Cpl Thew was on guard at his company headquarters in West Wickham when a bomb fell on a pair of houses in an adjoining road. Cpl Thew went immediately taking with him Volunteers L.

A. Piercy and H. J. Bartlett. He burrowed into a small hole in the debris and after working for some time when coal gas was escaping, managed to release a small girl who was wedged. He then returned to rescue two women with the assistance of the two Volunteers. He was informed that there were no persons in the adjoining house, but went to investigate and found a man, his wife and three children whom he helped out."

Beckenham Journal 28 February 1942

Lieutenant Colonel J. A. Thicknesse RA

Awarded the DSO for "four days skilful reconnaissance in a jeep. It was in an unmapped part of the Western Desert before the British lines so that the artillery could be directed at the most vital part of the enemy position. He dodged enemy armoured cars and one low flying ME 109 shot the front tyres of the jeep to pieces."

Bromley Mercury 19 March 1943

Staff Sergeant A. Tilley RASC

Mentioned in Despatches "for gallantry and distinguished service in NW Europe."

Beckenham Journal 1 June 1946

Pilot Officer Ronald W. Tuck RAFVR 21 Squadron

Awarded the DFC. ". . . completed many sorties against a variety of targets and has set a fine example of skill, courage and tenacity . . . On one occasion recently his aircraft was hit by A.A. fire. A large hole was torn in the fuselage, part of his mainplane was torn away, whilst the nose of the aircraft was badly damaged. Great physical exertion was necessary in order to maintain a measure of control, but P/O Tuck stuck resolutely to his task and succeded in flying the aircraft to an airfield in this country. He displayed skill and fortitude of a high order."

Beckenham Journal 1 July 1944

Major A. Waterman RE

Mentioned in Despatches for distinguished service.

Beckenham Journal 5 May 1945

Sergeant Frederick J. Watson 15 Squadron

Awarded an immediate DFM. "One night in July 1943 Sgt Watson was Flight Engineer of an aircraft detailed for an operation against Hamburg. When nearing the target engine trouble developed causing the bomber to vibrate violently. The defective engine caught fire and burned fiercely. In an effort to extinguish the flames by the force of the wind, the pilot dived the aircraft to 6,000 feet. His efforts were unsuccessful and it was not until the bomber was down to 2,500 feet that the flames were extinguished. Some height was then regained and the course set for home. When over the North Sea a second engine became defective and in order to maintain height all moveable equipment was jettisoned and thus the pilot was enabled to reach an airfield where he effected a safe landing. During the return flight Sgt Watson displayed great coolness and resource and assisted materially to the safe return of the aircraft. In very trying circumstances this member of aircraft crew displayed great courage, coolness and determination.''

Bromley Mercury 27 August 1943

Squadron Leader Gordon Wells
Appointed MBE (Military Division)

Kentish Times 15 March 1946

Flight Lieutenant Jack Wetherly 76 Squadron
Awarded the DFC

London Gazette 1 June 1945

Pilot Officer Lionel J. D. Wheble 635 Squadron
Awarded the DFC

London Gazette 15 September 1944

Appendix 1   Roll of Honour

ROYAL NAVY

ALEN: Sub Lt Peter. RNVR Fleet Air Arm *HMS Saker*. Killed in an accident at Fort Lauderdale USA 2 April 1944. Bur Woodlawn Park Cemetery Miami USA.

BRISTOW: Petty Officer Harold J. LT/KX 114344 RN Patrol Service. *HM Trawler Orfasy*. Kia 22 October 1943. Named on the Lowestoft Memorial Suffolk. Panel 12 Column 2.

GILROY: AB Stanley P/JX 187751 RN *HM Submarine Thunderbolt*. Kia 28 March 1943. Named on The Portsmouth Naval Memorial Hants. Panel 74 Column 3.

PLANNER: O/Seaman Gordon G. H. P/JX 252619 RN *HMS Belmont*. Kia 31 January 1942. Named on The Portsmouth Naval Memorial Hants. Panel 66 Column 1.

SHEEN: Petty Officer William J. D/JX 141174 RN *HMS Prince of Wales*. Kia 10 December 1941. Named on The Plymouth Naval Memorial Devon. Panel 45 Column 3.

SHOVE: O/Seaman Michael P. P/JX 275784 RN *HMS Belmont*. Kia 31 January 1942. Named on The Portsmouth Naval Memorial Hants. Panel 66 Column 1.

ARMY

BANKS: Private George. Irish Guards. Kia N Africa May 1943.

BELLRINGER: Cpl F. Arthur T/118234 198 Field Ambulance RASC. Shot dead while escaping from a prisoner-of-war camp in Thailand 16 November 1944. Bur Chungkai War Cemetery Thailand. Plot 11 Row G Grave 7.

BURNET: Cpl Cyril E. 7927885 'C' Sqn The Nottinghamshire Yeomanry, RAC. Kia 10 September 1944. Bur Gheele War Cemetery Belgium. Plot 1 Row B Grave 13.

BUSH: Lt Ronald G. W. 189375 5 Bn Hampshire Regt. Kia 23 February 1943. Bur Medjez-El-Bab War Cemetery Tunisia. Plot 5 Row F Grave 12.

CLERIHEW: Lt Clive H. P. 226375 2 Bn Rifle Brigade. Died of wounds 28 April 1943. Bur Massicault War Cemetery Tunisia. Plot 4 Row L Grave 16.

CLOUSTON: Cpl John W. 2013449 RE. Died of wounds 17 June 1944. Bur Hermanville War Cemetery. France. Plot 1 Row U Grave 12.

DILL: Lt John P. 2184 Men. in Desp. New Zealand Artillery. Died of wounds Crete 2 June 1941. Named on The Athens Memorial Greece. Face 12.

DURLING: L/Sgt Richard J. 6404956 1 Bn Royal Sussex Regt. Died of wounds 13 February 1944. Bur Cassino War Cemetery Italy. Plot 7 Row K Grave 3.

GARDNER: Gunner Leonard V. 6345522 3 Bty 6 HAA Regt. RA. Kia 13 February 1942. Named on The Singapore Memorial Singapore. Column 18.

GORDON: Lt Ronald E. J. 239423 1 Bn The London Scottish, The Gordon Highlanders. Kia 8 February 1944. Bur Anzio War Cemetery Italy. Plot 4 Row M Grave 5.

HALE: L/Cpl Edward C. 14326110 5 Bn Hampshire Regt. Kia 15 September 1944. Bur Gradara War Cemetery Italy. Plot 2 Row E Grave 23.

HEYWOOD: Sapper Rupert 1881197 RE. Died of wounds 11 August 1944. Bur Bayeux War Cemetery France. Plot 5 Row E Grave 16.

HOER: Rfmn Raymond K. 14419119 1 Bn Rifle Brigade. Kia 14 June 1944. Bur Bayeux War Cemetery France. Plot 15 Row J Joint Grave 13–14. Commemorated St. John's churchyard L36.

LAMBERT: L/Cpl Aubrey C. S/227628 RASC Attd HQ Malaya Command. Kia Sumatra 13 February 1942. Named on The Singapore Memorial Singapore. Column 99. Commemorated in St. John's churchyard L27.

LAVIS: Private Eric W. 6087032 2 Bn The Queen's Royal Regt. (West Surrey). Kia 26 June 1941. Bur Damascus Commonwealth War Cemetery Syria. Plot H Grave 4.

MASON: 2/Lt George F. A. 234307 MM 4th County of London Yeomanry (Sharpshooters) RAC. Kia 29 May 1942. Named on The Alamein Memorial Egypt. Column 29.

PIERCY: Lewis. Former Home Guard. Died while training with HM Forces February 1944. Bur St. John's churchyard 026.

SIMPSON: 2/Lt J.

SMITH: Signalman Royston A. 2327994 RCS, Guards Armoured Div Signals. Died of wounds 5 August 1944. Bur St. Charles de Percy War Cemetery France. Plot Row G. Grave 14. Commemorated St. John's churchyard K31.

THICKNESSE: Brigadier Henry J. A. DSO RA and Commands and Staff. Died of wounds in enemy hands 23 October 1944. Bur Dordrecht General Cemetery Netherlands. Row A Grave 3. Named on Hayes War Memorial.

TWYFORD: Wt Offr II (BSM) Charles L. 847536 146 (The Pembrokeshire Yeomanry) Field Regt. RA. Kia 29 March 1943. Bur Sfax War Cemetery Tunisia. Plot 3 Row C Grave 17.

WILSON: Cpl Harold O. 7934291 'A' Sqn 2nd Fife and Forfar Yeomanry, RAC formerly of 24th Lancers RAC. Kia 21 August 1944. Bur St. Desir War Cemetery France. Plot 2 Row E Grave 11.

ATS

COPPIN: Private Betty W/295412. Killed on active service 13 September 1944 at Dover. Bur St. John's churchyard P11.

ROYAL AIR FORCE

ALLCORN: Sergeant Ronald F. 131869 RAFVR. Killed 16 October 1943. Named on The Ottawa Memorial Canada. Panel 2 Column 2.

ANDREWS: F/Lt (W-Op) Ronald J. 105186 RAFVR 7 Squadron. Kia 20 January 1944. Bur Berlin 1939–1945 War Cemetery Germany. Plot 2 Row C Grave 20.

BARRON: Sergeant Jack.

BRADBROOK: Sergeant (Flt Engr) Lawrence H. 568805 RAF 405 RCAF Squadron. Kia 30 June 1942. Bur Reichswald Forest War Cemetery Cleves Germany. Plot 15 Row B Coll-grave 9–18.

CHARMAN: Sergeant/Pilot Peter J. 1381658 RAFVR 110 Squadron. Kia Burma 2 January 1944. Named on The Singapore Memorial Singapore. Column 436. Commemorated in St. John's churchyard D34.

CHUGG: Sergeant/Pilot Gordon E. 1291021. Killed in a flying accident 4 August 1941. Bur St. John's churchyard P110.

CULMER: Sergeant/Pilot Stanley 1283606 25 Squadron. Kia 14 April 1942. Bur St. John's churchyard P9.

CURTIS: Gordon.

DAVIES: F/Lt (Bomb Aimer) Richard E. 67648 RAFVR 61 Squadron. Kia 1 September 1943. Bur Streatham Park Cemetery Mitcham Surrey. Square 26 Grave 36708.

EDWARDS: F/Lt Geoffrey A. B. 142070 RAFVR. Kia Java 7 November 1945. Bur Djakarta War Cemetery Indonesia. Plot 5 Row J Grave 3.

FULLER: Pilot Officer (Bomb Aimer) Michael J. 143760 RAFVR 617 Squadron. Kia 17 May 1943. Bur Reichswald Forest War Cemetery Cleves Germany. Plot 5 Row B Coll-grave 16–18.

HOWARD: LAC John A. 1545132 RAFVR. Killed in a flying accident 31 March 1943. Bur Swift Current (Mount Pleasant) Cemetery Saskatchewan Canada. Block 2 Grave 4. Named on Old Mid-Whitgiftians' Memorial Board.

JAMES: Flying Officer (Pilot) Ross 42062 DFC RAF 35 Squadron. Kia 3 September 1941. Bur Berlin 1939–1945 War Cemetery Germany. Plot 4 Row J Joint grave 18–19.

JONES: Stanley W. Killed 21 April 1940.

LOVELAND: Sergeant/Flt Engnr Ambrose W. 1896159. Kia 25 September 1944. Bur St. John's churchyard B39.

MELLOWS: Lieutenant Harold S. 87329 RAFVR 115 Squadron. Killed on active service 11 November 1941. Bur Marham Cemetery Norfolk. War Graves Plot Grave 6.

O'CALLAGHAN: Flying Officer (Pilot) F. G. Denis 85495 RAFVR 277 Squadron. Kia 25 June 1944. South London Crematorium Mitcham Surrey. Panel 27.

PAGE: Flight Lieutenant Henry C. S. 41315 DFC 61 Squadron. Kia 31 January 1942. Bur Old Town Cemetery St. Mary's Scilly Isles.

PARRY: Sergeant/Pilot Gordon S. 1166710. Killed in a flying accident in Wales 28 July 1941. Bur St. John's churchyard P15.

PETERS: Flight Sergeant Bernard C. 1284019 RAFVR 249 Squadron. Kia 15 September 1942. Named on The Malta Memorial Malta. Panel 3 Column 2.

PETERS: Sergeant/Air Gunner Sydney A. 1375360. Killed 21 January 1942. Bur St. John's churchyard P8.

ROBERTS: Sergeant Michael F. 1337441 RAFVR 21 OTU. Kia 25 February 1943. Named on The Runnymede Memorial Egham Surrey. Panel 163.

ROSE: Flight Sergeant Donald 1418696 RAFVR 356 Squadron. Kia 13 June 1945 nr Bengal. Bur Maynamati War Cemetery Comilla Pakistan. Plot 3 Row B Grave 2.

RUSSELL: Flight Sergeant Frank A. 1282820. Kia 25 February 1945. Bur St. John's churchyard P24.

SHAYES: Sergeant/Pilot Ronald A. 934004 RAFVR 20 SFTS. Killed in a flying accident in Rhodesia 17 December 1940. Bur Harare (Pioneer) Cemetery Zimbabwe. European War Graves Plot Grave 16.

TILBURY: Sergeant/Pilot Kenneth J. 1323644 RAFVR 152 OTU. Killed on active service. Bur Karachi War Cemetery Pakistan. Plot 3 Row D Grave 11.

WEST: Sergeant/Pilot George W. 1384504. Killed in a flying accident 31 August 1942. Bur St. John's churchyard P23.

WETHERLY: Flight Lieutenant Jack H. 82716 DFC RAFVR 76 Squadron. Kia 30 March 1943. Bur Kiel War Cemetery Germany. Plot 4 Row J Grave 15.

WHITE: Sergeant/Pilot James B. 741288 RAFVR. Killed on active service. Bur St. John's churchyard P7. Named on Old Mid-Whitgiftians' Memorial Board.

WILLIAMS: Sergeant/Air Gunner Cyril 1396380. Killed 19 April 1944. Bur St. John's churchyard P10.

WRIGHT: Sergeant/Navigator John H. 1388972 RAFVR 102 Squadron. Kia 26 June 1943. Bur Bergen General Cemetery Netherlands. Plot 2 Row C Grave 4.

HOME GUARD

CHUDLEY: Cpl Arthur 55 Kent Bn. Died while on exercises 6 June 1943. Bur St. John's churchyard P21.

MERCHANT NAVY

JOHNSTON: Gordon H. Lost at sea. Commemorated St. John's churchyard P67.

CIVIL DEFENCE

AGATE: Ernest. Heavy Rescue. Killed 16 Jun 1944.

AITCHISON: Percy. AFS. Killed 19 Apr 1941.

BAILEY: Henry. Heavy Rescue. Killed 16 Jun 1944.

BEADLE: Ernest. AFS. Killed 19 Apr 1941. Bur St. John's K48.

BROWNE: Harold. Heavy Rescue. Killed 16 Jun 1944.

BURTON: Frank OBE. Heavy Rescue. Killed 16 Jun 1944.

CARDEN: H. C. AFS. Killed 19 Apr 1941.

DEANES: Robert J. AFS. Killed 19 Apr 1941.

DREW: C. Wesley. AFS. Killed 19 Mar 1941. Bur St. John's K47.

ELLIOTT: Albert H.

FARLEY: Cecil. AFS. Killed 19 Apr 1941.

FATHARLY: W.

FITZGERALD: Dennis G. AFS. Killed 19 Mar 1941. Bur St. John's K47.

LATHWOOD: Laurence. Heavy Rescue. Killed 16 Jun 1944.

MOORE: Frederick W. AFS. Killed 19 Mar 1941. Bur St. John's K47.

MOUNTJOY: Norman R. AFS. Killed 19 Apr 1941. Bur St. John's K48.

PALMER: Leslie. AFS. Killed 19 Mar 1941. Bur St. John's K47.

PARFETT: Martin. AFS. Killed 19 Apr 1941.

SHORT: Stanley. AFS. Killed 19 Mar 1941. Bur St. John's K47.

WINGHAM: George MM. Heavy Rescue. Killed 16 Jun 1944.

CIVILIANS

BAKER: Montagu A. Killed 2 Mar 1942. Bur St. John's A13.

BEVIS: James. Killed 15 Oct. 1940. Bur St. John's Q21.

BEVIS: Mary E. Killed 15 Oct 1940. Bur St. John's Q21.

BOYDEN: Albert. Killed 9 Sep 1940. Bur St. John's J119.

CLOUSTON: Doris. Killed 22 Mar 1944.
DRAY: Eliza. Killed 1 Oct 1940. Bur St. John's H33.
DRAY: Elsie C. L. Killed 1 Oct 1940. Bur St. John's H33.
DRAY: Percival. Killed 1 Oct 1940. Bur St. John's H33.
DULLEY: Kenneth. Killed 2 Mar 1942. Bur St. John's A13.
ELKINS: Alfred. Killed 12 Sep 1940. Bur St. John's L68.
ELKINS: Elizabeth. Killed 12 Sep 1940. Bur St. John's L68.
ELKINS: Gladys. Killed 12 Sep 1940. Bur St. John's L68.
EVANS: Oscar. Killed 14 Sep 1940. Bur St. John's M3.
EVANS: Thomas. Killed 14 Sep 1940. Bur St. John's M3.
FOTHERGILL: David. Killed 2 Mar 1942. Bur St. John's A13.
GALLOWAY: S.F.
GOODCHILD: Frank. Died of injuries 17 Jun 1944.
GOSLING: George. Killed 11 May 1941. Bur St. John's P6.
GOSLING: Hilda B. Killed 11 May 1941. Bur St. John's P6.
GOSLING: Victor. Died 21 Nov 1946 as a result of war injuries.
HAMMOND: Charles. Killed Sep 1940.
HOLT: R.K.
LINNETT: Joan Snr. Killed 11 May 1941.
LINNETT: Joan Jnr. Killed 11 May 1941.
LINNETT: William. Killed 11 May 1941.
LUCAS: D.
MARFLEET: Nora. Killed 5 Sep 1940. Bur St. John's A1.
MARFLEET: Vera. Killed 5 Sep 1940. Bur St. John's A1.
NICHOLLS: Frederick. Killed 11 May 1941.
NICHOLLS: Frances. Killed 11 May 1941.
NORMAN: Tyler. Killed 12 Jul 1944. Bur St. John's K3.
REYNOLDS: Walter. Killed 2 Aug 1944. Bur St. John's H82.
ROBBINS: Dorothy. Killed 2 Jan 1944. Bur St. John's P147.
SHARPE: Thomas W. Killed Jul 1944.
SINGLEHURST: Walter. Killed 19 Jul 1944. Bur St. John's K4.
SULLIVAN: Josephine. Killed 5 Sep 1940. Bur St. John's A1.
WAITE: David. Killed 13 Feb 1942 when *HMS Giang Bee* was sunk
  while evacuating refugees from Singapore.
WARD: ? Killed 15 Oct 1940.
WESTROPP: Frank. Killed 2 Mar 1942. Bur St. John's Q1.
WILKINS: Alan. Killed 2 Mar 1942.
WOOD: (Mrs). Killed 15 Oct 1940.

Appendix 2   Prisoners-of-War

ALLISON: Cpl Jack MM RCS. Germany 1944.
ANSCOMB: CPO Charles DSM RN. Italy 1942, Germany 1943.
  Escaped 1944.
BANFIELD: Sgt John K. RAF. Germany 1943.
BELLRINGER: Sgt Arthur RASC. Thailand 1942. Killed 1944.
BLAKE: Gunner C. W. S. Italy 1942.
BROOKS: Sapper Norman. Italy 1942.
CHAMBERS: F/O Kenneth RAF. Germany 1944.
CLARKE: L/Cpl Robert MM RB. Italy 1943.
COLLISTER: Sgt Stanley RAOC. Germany 1941.
COTTON: Telegraphist Walter D. In Japanese hands 1942.
CRIER: Cpl Jack RAF. Japan 1942.
DAVIS: Lt. Glider Pilot.
DAY: Eddie. In Japanese hands 1942.
FULLEX: Gunner Harold RA. Italy 1942.
GREEN: Signaller R. RCS. Germany 1944.
GURNEY: Bdr Alan RA. Italy 1942. Escaped 1944.
HARRISON: Sgt ? RAF. 1940.
HAWES: Sgt John RASC. Germany 1940.
HAYNES: Charles. Italy 1942.
HOLDER: Sgt F. W. RAOC. Italy 1942.
HUTCHINSON: Jack. Singapore 1942.
JONES: Gunner Leslie H. Singapore 1942, Thailand, Japan.
KEENOR: L/Bdr Frank RA. Singapore 1942 Thailand 1943.
LAUSTE: Mjr Leslie W. RAMC. Germany 1940.
LYNN/LYON: Sgt/Pilot Eric R. Germany 1941.
MACKINDER: LAC Hugh K. Java 1942.
PARSONS: Cpl Gerald RWKR. Germany 1940.
ROBERTS: Frederick C. In Japanese hands 1942.
SAUNDERS: Sgt/Rear Gunner John RAF. Germany 1943.
STEPHENSON: Lt. John C. Buffs. Germany 1940.
STUART: Trooper Donald F. C. 7/Tank Corps. Italy 1942.
THICKNESSE: Brigadier Henry DSO RA. Captured and died in
  enemy hands 1944.

WALKER: Guardsman William Coldstream Guards. Germany 1942.
WHARTON: AB Eric RN. Germany 1943.
WHEBLE: P/O Leonard D. DFC. Germany 1944.
WILLIS: Gunner Ernest RA. Italy 1942.

Notes

1. A temporary Wickham Common School was opened in the Coney Hall farm buildings in 1935.
2. Westminster Bank provided some facilities before and after the First World War.
3. *Beckenham Journal* 5 March 1938
4. *Beckenham Journal* 8 January 1938
5. *Beckenham Journal* 19 March 1938
6. *Beckenham Journal* 26 March 1938
7. *Beckenham Journal* 24 September 1938
8. Letter to author from Miss Mercia Sansom
9. *Beckenham Journal* 9 September 1939
10. Ibid.
11. Ibid.
12. Michael P. O. Connor *St. David's College 1926-1986* St. David's College 1986
13. Letter to author from Mrs. Audrey Hearne *née* Thompson
14. Letter to author
15. Information from Bert Purkiss
16. Conversation with Oliver Woodman
17. Joyce Walker *West Wickham and the Great War* Hollies Publications 1988
18. Original designation. Not styled 55 Kent Bn Home Guard until March 1941
19. Conversation with the late Mrs. Ada James
20. Norman Gelb *Scramble. A Narrative History of the Battle of Britain* Michael Joseph 1986
21. Letter to author
22. Conversation with Alan Nelson
23. Anon. *Rapid Fire. An Account of some of the Happenings of 'D' Machine-Gun Company 55 Kent Bn Home Guard 1940-44* Typescript in Bromley Central Library archives
24. Ibid.
25. Ibid.
26. Letter to author
27. Letter to author from Miss Mercia Sansom
28. *Wickham Common Jubilee 1937-1987*
29. Letter to author from Miss Mercia Sansom
30. Ibid.
31. Ibid.

32. Letter to author
33. Ida Watson papers in Bromley Central Library
34. Letter to author
35. An excavation in 1990 resulted in finding three pieces of the engine in good condition, and the prop boss. The largest piece of the engine has been donated to the Polish Museum in London.
36. *London Gazette* 24 January 1941
37. Conversation with Bert Purkiss
38. Greenhayes School archives
39. Conversation with author
40. Destroyed by enemy action 16 April 1941
41. Conversation with author
42. Letter from Mrs. Connie Winter
43. Letter to author
44. Conversation with author
45. The crash site on the farm was excavated in 1985 and the surviving remains unearthed. The complete radio, taken at the time of the crash, was donated to Tangmere Aviation Museum.
46. Conversation with author
47. Letter to author from Mrs. Irene Roe
48. Ibid.
49. Letter to author
50. Letter to author
51. Letter to author
52. Alistair Macdonald *Langley Park Golf Club 1910–1985* Langley Park Golf Club Ltd. 1985
53. Greenhayes School archives
54. *Rapid Fire* op. cit.
55. Ibid.
56. Letter to author from Mrs. Pauline James *née* Parry
57. *Bromley Times* 2 January 1942
58. Conversation with Bob Squires
59. Hawes Down Junior School Log 22 October 1942
60. *Beckenham & Penge Advertiser* 5 August 1943
61. *London Gazette* 18 July 1944
62. Letter to author
63. Ida Watson papers in Bromley Central Library archives
64. Ibid.
65. Conversation with author
66. *Beckenham & Penge Advertiser* 22 June 1944
67. Letter to author
68. Letter to author
69. Conversation with author
70. Letter to author
71. Ida Watson papers in Bromley Central Library archives
72. Conversation with author
73. Letter to author

74. Ibid.
75. *Beckenham Journal* 17 March 1945
76. *Beckenham Journal* 11 August 1945
77. *Beckenham Journal* 29 September 1945
78. The author would welcome any additions to the Roll of Honour

Bibliography

PRIMARY

Beckenham Journal
Beckenham & Penge Advertiser
Beckenham Borough Council Minutes
Beckenham Urban District Council Minutes
Bromley Mercury
Bromley Times
Private and official correspondence concerning Cpl Jack Crier
Emmanuel Church Registers
Greenhayes School archives
Hawes Down Junior School Log Book
Hawes Down Senior School Log Book
Hawes Lane Methodist Church archives
Lecture Hall Charity – Trustees Minutes
London Gazette
Militärgeographische Angaben über England – London Berlin 1941
Register of electors 1939–1940
St. Catherine's House registers
St. Francis of Assisi Church West Wickham. Parish registers and other documents.
St. John the Baptist Church West Wickham. Parish registers and Directory of Graves.
St. Mary of Nazareth West Wickham. Parish registers
Ida Watson papers in Bromley Central Library archives

SECONDARY

Ralph Barker. *Children of the Benares.* Methuen 1987
Lewis Blake. *Before the War.* Lewis Blake 1985
Lewis Blake. *Bromley in the Front Line.* Revised print Lewis Blake 1983
Douglas Cluett, Joanna Bogle, Bob Learmouth. *Croydon Airport & the Battle for Britain 1939-40.* London Borough of Sutton Libraries & Art Services 1984
Richard Collier. *Eagle Day.* J. M. Dent & Sons Ltd 1980
Michael P. O. Connor. *St. David's College 1926-1986.* St. David's College 1986

135

Alan W. Cooper. *The Men who breached the Dams*. Wm Kimber 1987

Dr. Ronald Cox. *From Cradle to Conscription: A Schoolboy in Suburbia 1924-42*. Private publication

Bernard Darwin. *War on the Line - The S.R. in Wartime*. S.R. 1946

Len Deighton. *Battle of Britain*. Jonathan Cape Ltd 1980

Cyril Demarne. *The London Blitz - A Fireman's Tale*. Newham Parents' Centre 1980

John Foreman. *Battle of Britain. The Forgotten Months*. Air Research Publications 1988

Front Line 1940-1941. HMSO 1942

Norman Gelb. *Scramble. A Narrative History of the Battle of Britain*. Michael Joseph 1986

Elizabeth Gibbs. *Our Grand National*. Typescript

Benny Green (ed). *Wisden Anthology 1940-1963*. Macdonald 1985

Greystones 1911-1963. Private publication

Christopher Harris. *West Wickham 1880-1980*. Bromley Public Library 1983

A. M. Hayes. *Peace and War in Elmers End, Beckenham* 1981

Carlton Jackson. *Who will take our children*. Methuen 1980

E. S. Jeffries. *A Short History of the West Wickham Allotments Association 1912-1975*. Typescript

Marcel Jullian. *The Battle of Britain*. Jonathan Cape Ltd 1967

Kent Aviation Historical Research Society. *Kent Airfields in the Battle of Britain*. Meresborough Books 1981

Patricia Knowlden & Joyce Walker. *West Wickham - Past into Present*. Hollies Publications 1986

M. Leale. *Glebe House*. Private publication

Peter Lewis. *A People's War*. Methuen 1986

Alex Liddell. *Story of the Girl Guides 1938-1975*. Girl Guide Association 1976

Norman Longmate. *The Real Dad's Army*. Arrow Books 1974

Norman Longmate. *The Doodlebugs*. Hutchinson 1981

Norman Longmate (ed.). *The Home Front*. Chatto & Windus 1981

Norman Longmate. *Hitler's Rockets*. Hutchinson 1985

Alistair Macdonald. *Langley Park Golf Club 1910-1985*. Langley Park Golf Club Ltd 1985

Joanna Mack and Steve Humphries. *The Making of Modern London 1939-1945*. Sidgwick & Jackson 1985

The Metropolitan Police at War. HMSO 1947

Raynes Minns. *Bombers and Mash*. Virago Press

Bob Ogley. *Biggin on the Bump*. Froglet Publications 1990

John Player. *A History of the Warren*. Private publication

Winston G. Ramsey (ed.). *The Blitz - Then and Now*. Vol 1 Battle of Britain Prints International Ltd. 1987

Winston G. Ramsey (ed.). *The Blitz - Then and Now*. Vol 2 Battle of Britain Prints International Ltd. 1988

Winston G. Ramsey (ed.). *The Blitz - Then and Now*. Vol 3 Battle of Britain Prints International Ltd. 1990

Rapid Fire An account of some of the happenings of 'D' Machine-Gun Company 55 Kent Bn Home Guard 1940-1944. Private publication 1946
Roof over Britan. HMSO 1943
J. D. Sainsbury. *Hazardous Work.* Hart Books 1985
W. C. Berwick Sayers. *Croydon and the Second World War.* Croydon Corporation 1949
Eric Taylor. *Women who went to War 1938-1946.* Robert Hale 1988
Joyce Walker. *British Red Cross Society 1870-1970.* Private publication
Joyce Walker. *West Wickham and the Great War.* Hollies Publications 1988
Jane Waller and Michael Vaughan Rees. *Women in Wartime.* Macdonald Optima 1987
50 Active Years 1934-1984. 3rd West Wickham Scout Group Private publication
West Wickham Residents Association Year Book 1939
West Wickham South Residents Association Jubilee Newsletter Summer 1984
Charles Whiting. *The Three Star Blitz.* Leo Cooper 1987
Wickham Common School Jubilee 1937-1987. Private publication
Jack F. Wilson. *The Royal Observer Corps.* Typescript
Eric Wilton. *Centre Crew. A Memory of the Royal Observer Corps.* Private publication
Trevor Woodman. *The Railways to Hayes.* Hayes Village Association 1982
Kenneth G. Wynn. *Men of the Battle of Britain.* Gliddon Books 1989

CONVERSATIONS AND CORRESPONDENCE WITH:

Mrs. Alice Abbott
Mrs. Sarah Becket
Mr. Colin Brown
Mr. Harry Cannon
Mrs. Jean Chamberlain *née* Colley
Revd. Arthur L. Chambers
Mrs. Elizabeth Chapman
Mr. Richard Charman
Mr. Jack Clear
Mrs. Ivy Cleobury
Mr. Alan Connolly
Dr. Ronald Cox
Mrs. Ivy Crier
Mr. Arthur Davie
Mr. Thomas Durrell
Mr. Colin Edmeads
Mrs. Margaret Edmeads
Mr. Kenneth Gaved
Mrs. Elizabeth Gibbs
Mr. Gerald Gordon
Mrs. Winifred Gordon
Mrs. Kathleen Hart

Mrs. Audrey Hearne *née* Thompson
Miss Rose Hobson
Mrs. Mary Hogg
Mrs. Eileen Horan *née* Rogers
Mrs. Ada James
Mrs. Pauline James *née* Parry
Mrs. Emily Kilby
Mr. & Mrs. John Lawson
Mrs. Margaret Mayes *née* Balaam
Mrs. Doreen Meloy *née* Killick
Mr. W. John Merigan
Mrs. Joyce Moore
Mrs. Florrie Morse *née* Fullex
Miss Marjorie Moyce
Mr. Alan Nelson
Mrs. Lilian Pain
Mrs. Eileen Preston
Mr. Frank Preston
Mr. Herbert Purkiss
Mrs. Ada Raymond
Revd. George Raymond MBE
Mrs. Irene Roe
Miss Mercia Sansom
Mrs. Marjorie Scudamore
Miss Muriel Searle
Mr. Alfred Sheen
Mrs. Kathleen Sheridan
Mrs. Christine Squires
Mr. Robert Squires
Miss Joan Walker
Mr. Ron Warner
Mr. Ken Wills
Mrs. Dorothy Wingent
Mrs. Connie Winter *née* Manser
Mrs. Gwen Woodman
Mr. Oliver Woodman

Index

Note: The figures in *italic* refer to illustrations

144

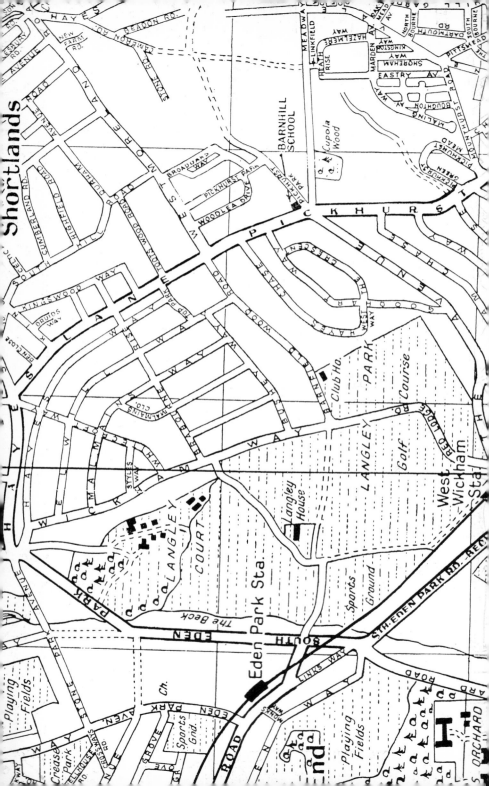